CONTENTS

Introduction

****

INTRODUCTION

This latest edition to the Easyway Guides Series, A Guide to Copyright and Intellectual Property Law, Revised edition, updated to **2021,** deals comprehensively and clearly with a complex, elusive and rapidly changing area, of importance to those engaged in the commercial world, or to teachers of the subject. The book deals with the UK and makes reference to differences in the ways of dealing with disputes in Scotland and Northern Ireland.

What differentiates the book from others in the field is that it is written in such a way that it is of benefit to students of law and those who wish to gain a practical understanding of the subject area.

The law of intellectual property impinges upon the lives of many people, whether traders, artists, musicians or designers. Whatever we do, whatever we create, we need to understand what protection the law affords our endeavours. This brief book introduces the reader to the meaning of intellectual property and deals in depth with the various aspects of intellectual property such as:

-Patents and patent law, protecting the inventor
-Confidential information and breach of confidence
-Trademarks, distinguishing one trader's goods from another
-Passing off, appropriating and damaging goodwill
-Character merchandising,
-Copyright and infringement of copyright
-design rights.
-Computer software.

The book has a dual function, firstly as an introduction n to the law and secondly it has been updated to include the practical process of how to apply for patents, trade marks and registered designs. The chapter on protection of computer software has been updated and also a new section on other forms of IP protection has been included. In 2014, the Intellectual Property Act was introduced, along with other regulations affecting both copyright and also deign rights. These are fully outlined in relevant chapters.

In addition, changes to patent rules, which came into force on October 1st 2016, and also April 2017, will be outlined. Also, From 14 January 2019 the long-awaited Trade Mark Directive (2015/2436) took effect in the UK which reflected the UK's continued effort to enhance harmonisation of trade mark law across the EU. This has now been affected by BREXIT, see below.

BREXIT and Intellectual Property Law

It is important to note the many changes to IP law following the outcome of the BREXIT negotiations, and final withdrawal on January 1st 2021. The changes affecting each area of Intellectual property will be outlined at the beginning of the relevant chapters.

****

Ch. 1

Intellectual Property

Introduction and Summary

Intellectual property is an area of law which is complex and rapidly changing. *Intellectual property rights* is the overall term used to describe the various rights that afford protection to creative and innovative endeavour. There are a number of main rights, described in more detail throughout the book, including the following:

- Patents. This is a statutory property right that gives the patent holder the exclusive right to use certain inventions. A patent can be obtained by application to the Intellectual Property Office. Many people or organisations will use an agent to obtain a patent but it can be done on a do-it-yourself basis more cheaply. A patent will typically last up to twenty years.
- Trademarks. A registered trademark is, like a patent, a statutory right and gives the exclusive right to use a distinctive sign in relation to either a product or service. The sign can be a name, a symbol, aroma, jingle etc. A trademark can be obtained via an application to the Intellectual Property Office. A trademark may be renewed indefinitely. Again, agents are used in the process but it can be carried out on a DIY basis.
- Copyright and moral rights. Copyright is a statutory right subsisting in original literary, dramatic, musical and

artistic works and in sound recordings, films, broadcasts, cable programs and the typography of published editions. Owners of copyright will have economic rights within their works, including the important right to prevent unauthorised copying and adaptation. Moral rights are rights that authors retain in their works, irrespective of who owns the economic rights. Copyright varies according to its life span, usually the life of an author plus seventy years. Moral rights are personal to the author and arise automatically.

- Breach of confidence. The action for breach of confidence can be used to protect certain categories of confidential information, such as commercial information against unauthorised use or disclosure. The origins are contractual or equitable and the duration is indefinite or until the information is released into the public domain.

- Passing off. Goodwill is a form of property constituting the markets perception of the value and quality of a business and its products. This can be protected against interference or damage by what is known as 'passing off'. This is a tort that may be used in preventing a trader from making misrepresentations, which damages the goodwill of another trader. Again this is indefinite but ceases when the goodwill of a particular enterprise ceases.

- Design law. Certain aspects of the appearance of articles, aesthetic or non-aesthetic are protected via a combination of the registered design system, the design right (an unregistered design system) and aspects of copyright law. A registered design is the exclusive right to use certain features of a range of products. A design right is the right to prevent the copying of aspects of the shape or configuration of an article, such as a certain type of car. An unregistered design right will last up to fifteen years. A registered design, which can be granted upon application to the Intellectual Property Office, can last up to twenty five years, but must be renewed at 5 yearly intervals.

Infringement of intellectual property rights

The holder of an intellectual property right has to be in a position to enforce his or her rights if there is found to be an infringement of the IPR. In the main, civil remedies are available. However, certain infringements constitute a criminal offence. Remedies available after trial are known as final remedies. Interim remedies are also available, which are remedies awarded during trial. In relation to final remedies, financial remedies may take the form of damages or an account of profits. Examples of IP infringement include when someone:

- Uses, sells or imports a patented product or process
- Uses all or some of another's work under copyright without their permission
- Makes, offers or sells someone's registered design for commercial gain
- Uses a trade mark that's identical or similar to one another has registered

The following steps can be taken:

- Get the other party to stop using IP or come to an agreement with them, for example license the IP.
- Use mediation or another type of dispute resolution.

- Take legal action if parties can't resolve the dispute by other means.

Report IP crime

It can be a criminal offence to copy or use copyright material and registered trade marks and designs without permission. Suspected IP crime should be reported to Trading Standards by contacting Citizens Advice.

Get help and advice

An intellectual property (IP) professional can give legal advice on a dispute, or act on someone's behalf. An IP professional can be found through organisations including:

- The Chartered Institute of Patent Attorneys
- The Chartered Institute of Trade Mark Attorneys
- The Law Society (England and Wales)
- The Law Society of Scotland
- The Law Society of Northern Ireland

Contact the Intellectual Property Office (IPO)

A person can contact IPO for:

- an opinion on whether their patent or supplementary protection certificate is being infringed - it costs £200
- to start legal proceedings over some types of IP dispute
- general advice on IP

Come to an agreement

If someone is using a person's IP without their permission they can contact them and ask them to stop.

Make a deal

A person can offer to make a deal with the other party, which is usually cheaper and quicker than going to court. They can also come to a Coexistence Agreement with someone who has a similar trade mark. A coexistence agreement is a legal agreement whereby two parties agree to trade in the same or similar market using an identical or similar trade mark.

Use a mediator

A person can use a mediator if they can't come to an agreement over an intellectual property (IP) dispute. Mediation is a way of resolving disputes without going to court. It's cheaper and quicker than taking legal action and the outcome is usually beneficial to all parties. Mediators provide an independent view on a dispute. They can't make a decision for another person, but they can help to find a solution that both parties accept. Discussions with a mediator are confidential and can't be used in court later if the dispute isn't resolved. Mediation can be used in most IP disputes including those about infringement, licensing, and patent entitlement.

IPO mediation service

The Intellectual Property Office (IPO) has its own mediation service. What someone will pay for mediation depends on how much time they need and the approximate value of the claim.

Other mediators

Civil Mediation Council (England and Wales)
Scottish Mediation Network
Northern Ireland Mediation

Take legal action

A person can file legal proceedings either through the Intellectual Property Office (IPO) or through the courts. Some types of proceedings can only be filed through one or the other. A court will expect a person to have tried to resolve their dispute - possibly using mediation - before starting legal proceedings.

File through the courts in England and Wales

The court to go to depends on the nature, complexity and value of a claim.

Claims below £10,000

A person can use the Intellectual Property Enterprise Court (IPEC) small claims track if their claim is for less than £10,000 and for infringement of one of the following:

copyright
passing off
trade marks
breach of confidence
unregistered design rights

A lawyer isn't needed to use the IPEC small claims track.

Claims up to £500,000

A person can take a case for any IP right to the Intellectual Property Enterprise Court (IPEC) if they do not wish to claim more than:

£50,000 for legal costs

£500,000 for damages

If someone is claiming more than £500,000 in damages

They use the Chancery Division of the High Court of England and Wales - there are no limits to legal costs or damages they can claim.

File through the courts in Scotland

Court of Session should be used if a claim is complex or valuable - there are no limits to legal costs or damages one can claim.

File through the courts in Northern Ireland

A person can use the Chancery Division of the High Court of Northern Ireland if their claim is complex or valuable - there are no limits to legal costs or damages one can claim.

****

Ch. 2

Patents and the Law

Historical background to patents and patent law

Patents were originally granted by the Crown exercising its Royal Prerogative. Letters patents were a royal proclamation that the bearer had the Crown's authority to do whatever had been authorised within the letters. The earliest record of a granted patent dates from 1331, to a Flemish weaver who wanted to practice his trade in England. Most of the patents granted at the time were to encourage trade rather than new inventions. In many cases, the grant of a patent was a way of controlling trade and towards the end of Elizabeth 1's reign, there were many abuses of the system.

The Statute of Monopolies 1623 was passed to control or limit these abuses. Monopolies per se were excluded unless they came within the exception in s.6. Under s.6 a 14-year monopoly could be granted for 'any manner of new manufacture'. The Patents Act 1835 was passed to deal with disclaimers and prolongations of claim, but the first comprehensive statute on the subject was the Patent Law Amendment Act 1852 which set up the Patent Office and Registrar of Patents. The Act also introduced the important requirement that a 'specification' be filed with an application describing the nature of the invention.

In 1883, the Patents, Designs and Trade Marks Act was passed to enable the United Kingdom to satisfy its obligations of reciprocity under the Paris Convention for the protection of Industrial Property. This Act required a full specification including detailed claims to be completed by the applicant and examined by the Patent Office before a patent would be granted. The case of Nobel's Explosive Company Limited v Anderson (1894) established that it was no longer possible to claim that the patent extended to matter contained within the specification where such matter was not in the claim. This highlighted the use of claims to mark the legal boundaries of the claim.

At this point in time, the United Kingdom patenting system was purely a deposit system, where applications were checked simply to make sure they had been completed correctly. The need to prove that an invention was really new did not come until the passing of the Patents Act 1907 which introduced the practice of checking patents for novelty, with searches being extended to cover patents granted over the last 50 years. The grounds for declaring a patent invalid were codified in the 1907 Act. In the 1919 Patents Act it was stated that invalid claims within an application would not invalidate the whole application.

The entire patents system was overhauled in 1949 by the Patents Act 1949, and the modern law on patents is set down in the Patents Act 1977, as amended by:

-   the Copyright Design and Patents Act 1988
-   the Patents and Trade Marks (World Trade Organisation) Regulations 1999
-   the Patents Regulations 2000
-   the Enterprise Act 2002
-   the Regulatory Reform (Patents Order) 2004
-   the Patents Act 2004
-   the Medicines (Marketing Authorisations etc.) Amendment Regulations 2005

- the Intellectual Property (Enforcement, etc.) Regulations 2006
- the Patents (Compulsory Licensing and Supplementary Protection Certificates) Regulations 2007
- the Legal Services Act 2007
- the Crime and Courts Act 2013 the Enterprise and Regulatory Reform Act 2013(Competition) (Consequential, Transitional and Saving Provisions) Order 2014
- the Copyright (Public Administration) Regulations 2014
- the Intellectual Property Act 2014
- the Legislative Reform (Patents) Order 2014, and the Patents (Supplementary Protection Certificates) Regulations 2014. The Intellectual Property Act 2014 became law from October 2014 and was fully implemented by the end of 2015. Key changes to patent law include:

- marking patented products with a web address
- expansion of the patent opinions service
- patents worksharing

Finally, the Intellectual Property (Unjustified Threats) Act 2017, which came into effect on 1st October 2017.

Patents in the context of BREXIT
Necessary amendments to UK national legislation have been enacted in the form of The Patents (Amendment) (EU Exit) Regulations 2019. You can apply for a European patent through the IPO or direct to the European Patent Office (EPO) to protect your patent in more than 30 countries in Europe, using the (non-

EU) European Patent Convention (EPC). As the EPO is not an EU agency, leaving the EU does not affect the current European patent system. Existing European patents covering the UK are also unaffected. European patent attorneys based in the UK continue to be able to represent applicants before the EPO.

In another change, the UK's address for service rules are changing. From 1 January 2021, the rules will not permit the provision of an address for service outside the UK, the Channel Islands or Gibraltar in respect of a UK patent (GB or EP(UK)) or an application in the UK IPO. The provision of an address for service in the remaining EU or EEA will no longer be permitted. New patent applications filed in the UK IPO from 1 January 2020 will need to comply with the new regime. There will be transitional provisions for applications and proceedings that remain pending on 1 January 2021. The legislative amendments are contained in The Patents, Trade Marks and Designs (Address for Service) (Amendment) (EU Exit) Rules 2020 (SI 2020/1317).

Supplementary Protection Certificates

A supplementary protection certificate (SPC) is a form of intellectual property that extends patent term in respect of medicinal or plant protection products in qualifying circumstances. The maximum duration of an SPC is five years, which is intended to compensate, to some degree, for the period elapsing between the filing of an application for a patent for a new medicinal or plant protection product and the grant of authorisation to place the medicinal product or plant protection product on the market. The term of SPC protection in respect of a medicinal product may be extended by six months (a 'paediatric extension') if certain criteria are satisfied.

SPCs are granted as national rather than EU-wide rights. It was not necessary for the UK and the EU to agree the creation of a comparable right to ensure continued protection of existing SPCs in the UK at the end of the transition period.

The Withdrawal Agreement ensures that SPC applications which are pending at the end of the transition period will be examined under the current framework. Any SPC which is granted based on those applications will provide the same protection as existing SPCs. You will continue to apply for an SPC by submitting an application to the Intellectual Property Office.

Changes affecting SPCs due to the Northern Ireland Protocol
Due to regulatory changes for marketing authorisations there are some changes to the SPC application process which will come into effect from 1 January. You will need to check whether your marketing authorisation is valid for the whole of the UK, or just Northern Ireland or Great Britain. An application for an SPC must still be filed with the IPO within six months of your first authorisation.

*

In this book, we are covering the essence of patents and the law covered by the 1977 Act as amended plus making reference to the Intellectual Property (Unjustified Threats) Act 2017.

The meaning of 'patent'
As we saw earlier, a patent is a monopoly right. The product or process, which is being patented, must first satisfy the criteria of the Patents Act 1977, which are:

1. There must be an invention, which must be capable of being patented but not an 'as such' invention. Certain

inventions are non-patentable. This arises out of the Patents Act 1977 s1 (2) and (3)) The statute does not provide a clear definition of invention but the Patents Act sets out a list of things that are considered to be inventions 'as such': general abstract entities, aesthetic and non-technical things are considered to be excluded. Discoveries, scientific theories and other things such as mathematical methods are not considered to be inventions 'as such'.

One of the most problematic areas to arise out of this definition of things that are not regarded as being true inventions is that of computer programs. Despite not being considered inventions under the PA 1977 it is the case that patents for software related inventions are indeed granted. Software patents are granted when a substantial technical contribution is made, as this is not considered to be a computer program as such. One of several approaches is taken when deciding whether there has been a technical contribution:

- The question should be asked whether technical means are used to produce a result or solve a problem
- Does the invention produce a technical result
- Novelty must be present in the product or process which distinguishes it from other products and processes (PA 1977 s.2)
- An inventive step must be present, i.e. the product or process must be seen as containing an clear element of invention (PA 1977 s. 3)

- The invention must be capable of industrial application, i.e. must be of a purpose which can be applied to some form of industry (PA 1977 s.4)

Other areas of enterprise are not patentable 'as such'. Mental acts, schemes, rules playing a game or business methods.

Mental acts. In Raytheon (1993) an apparatus and process was claimed for the identification of ships. This involved the digital composition of the silhouette of the unknown ship with silhouettes of known ships, held in a computer memory. The claim was held to be excluded as it was merely an automation of a method normally carried out by individuals, i.e. a mental act as such. Carrying out the method with a computer did not create a technical effect.

Schemes, rules or methods for playing a game. Innovations in this area do not really amount to a technical contribution.

Business methods. The courts in the UK have always taken a strict approach to the patentability of business methods. Inventions must make a technical contribution but that contribution must not be in an excluded thing (such as a business method) and it is also seen that advances in business methods are not technical. More recent European patent office developments indicate that a more relaxed approach may be adopted. Whilst process claims to business methods are not inventions, 'as such' product claims may be patentable.

The presentation of information

The Patents Act 1977 s.1 (2)(d) provides that means of presenting information are not inventions 'as such'.

Non-Patentable Inventions

In some cases, rare though they may be, the commercial exploitation of an invention may be contrary to public policy or morality. Such an invention is unpatentable. The European Patent Office in Harvard/Onco-mouse (1991) when considering the patentability of a mouse or other non-human mammal genetically engineered so as to be predisposed to develop cancer, suggested that this should be addressed as a balancing exercise. Here the suffering of the mouse and the possible environmental risks were felt to be outweighed by the utility of the invention to humans, hence the Onco-mouse was not immoral.

As public policy and morality objections proved particularly problematic in the field of biotechnology, Directive 09/44/EC on the legal protection of Biological Invention provides further guidance on what is not patentable:

- The formation and development of the human body and mere discoveries of elements of the human body (this includes gene sequences) are not patentable. However, where a technical process is used to isolate or produce elements (including genes) from the human body, this may be patentable.
- Processes for modifying human germ line genetic identity (i.e. genetic changes that can be passed to the next generation.
- Human cloning processes.
- Genetic engineering of animals which is likely to cause the animal to suffer without a substantial medical benefit, either to man or to animals.

- Plant or animal varieties or biological processes for the production of such varieties are not patentable, but inventions concerning plants or animals may be patented where the invention is not confined to a particular variety.

The concept of novelty

As discussed earlier, an invention must be novel (Patents Act 1977 s.1(1)(a) In UK patent law the terms 'novelty' and 'anticipation' are used interchangeably.

An invention must be new in the sense that it must not previously have been made available to the public. The Patents Act 1977 s.2 (1) provides that an invention is novel where it does not form part of the state of the art. Anticipation is judged by asking 'is the invention part of the state of the art'? Novelty is assessed objectively. In order for an invention to be anticipated, the prior art must either contain an enabling disclosure (in the case of a product patent) or, for process patents, it must give clear and unmistakable directions to do what the applicant has invented.

A key case here is Lux Traffic Controls Ltd v Pike Signals Ltd (1993) concerning what use amounts to disclosure to the public.. It was claimed that a temporary traffic signal was not 'new' because it had bee made available to the public in a paper, by oral disclosure, and by the use of a prototype which had been tested in public in Somerset.

The main principle to emerge from the case was that a prior publication must contain clear and unmistaken directions to do what the patentee claims to have invented: a signpost will not suffice. Where prior use is concerned there is no need for a skilled person to actually examine the invention as long as they were free in law and equity to do so and if a skilled person had seen it they would have been able to understand what the inventive concept was.

State of the art

The Patents Act 1977 s.2 (2) defines the state of the art as comprising all matter made available to the public before the priority date of the invention, this being the date of the first patent application. It therefore comprises all knowledge, global, on the subject matter of the invention. This knowledge can be made available in any way, either written, orally, or by any other means before the priority date.

The state of the art includes matter included in earlier patent applications, including those patent applications that are not yet published. Everything in the state of the art is known as prior art. Novelty destroying prior art could include information that is part of common general knowledge as well as specific pieces of prior art.

In some circumstances, a known invention may still be patented where a new use for that invention can be found, for example first medical use (Patents Act 1977) which provides that the first medical use of a known compound is novel, providing that the medical application of the compound does not itself form part of the state of the art (s.2 (6). Also second medical use. In Europe a policy has developed of allowing second and subsequent uses of known compounds. Such claims are novel where the second or subsequent medical use does nor form part of the state of the art and provided the patent application takes a very narrow form known as a Swiss Form Claim i.e. the use of medicament X for treatment of disease Y. The UK courts have sanctioned the use of Swiss Form Claims, but second and subsequent medical uses will only be novel in the UK, where there is a new therapeutic application, discovering information about a medical use is sufficient.

The Inventive step

An invention that is patentable must involve an inventive step. An inventive step is present where an invention would not be obvious to a person skilled in the art. In patent law, the term's 'inventive step' and 'non-obviousness' are used interchangeably.

Inventive steps are assessed from the perspective of the person skilled in the art (PA 1977 s.3), the skilled man. This hypothetical person has certain attributes, he is the average person in the relevant art, possessing the relevant skills, knowledge and qualifications. The statutory test for inventive step is embodied in what is know as the 'windsurfer' test. This test follows the approach set out in Windsurfer v Tabur Marine (1983) as modified by PLG Research Ltd v Ardon International Ltd (1995). According to the Windsurfer test, to test obviousness the following should be asked:

1. What is the inventive step involved in the patent?
2. At the priority date, what was the state of the art relevant to that test?
3. How does the step differ from the state of the art?
4. Without hindsight, would the taking of the step be obvious to the person skilled in the art?
5. When attempting to obtain a patent, it is important to note that patents are territorial rights, not universal and therefore it is necessary to apply for patents in each jurisdiction for which protection is desired. For example, a UK patent may be obtained from the Intellectual

Property Office. Although there is currently no 'European Patent' as such, a so called 'bundle' of patents, national patents, from states that are party to the European Patents Convention 1973 (EPC) may be obtained by a single patent application to the European Patent Office.

The employee inventor – ownership of patents

When a patent is applied for, the basic rules are that a patent must be granted to the following:

1) The inventor or joint inventors i.e. the actual devisor of the invention. (Patent Act 1977 s.7(2) (a)
2) The inventor(s) successors in title
3) The employer of an employee inventor.

Ownership of employee inventions

Inventors have the right to be mentioned as such but the Patent Act 1977 provides that where the inventors are employees their employer will own the invention if:

a) The invention was made in the course of the employee's normal duties or in the course of specially assigned duties, provided that he or she might reasonably be expected to carry out those duties.

b) Where the employee has a special obligation to further the interests of his employer's undertaking. This is related to the duty of fidelity that the employer owes to his or her employer.

Where the invention belongs to the employer, statutory compensation of the employer inventor may be available (PA 1977 s.40) provided that the patent is of outstanding benefit to the employer, the invention is subject of a patent grant and that it is just that compensation should be awarded.

There is a very high ceiling for statutory compensation and there has never actually been a reported case where statutory compensation under the 1977 act has been awarded. This is because such disputes tend to be settled out of court.

Patent applications may fail or those that are granted may be withdrawn on the basis of what is known as 'sufficiency'. A patent application consists of a number of components, and the patent specification is a vital part in which the invention is described and defined, it is the source of all the information about the patent that reaches the public domain. The specification must disclose the invention in such a way that the invention could be performed by the person skilled in the art. In other words, the application must contain an enabling disclosure.

The patent claim itself determines the scope of the monopoly granted to a patent proprietor. Claims must be clear and concise, be supported by the description and relate to a single inventive concept (PA 1977 s.14 (5).

Infringement of a patent

Certain activities carried out in the United Kingdom without permission of the patent holder constitute infringement (Section 60(1) and (2) of the Patents Act 1977:

1. Primary infringement. This falls into three categories:
    i)   where a product patent is at issue, making, disposing of, using, importing or keeping the patented product (or disposal or otherwise)

ii)   where a process patent is at issue, use of the process with actual or constructive knowledge that non-consensual use constitutes infringement

iii)   The use, offer to dispose of, importation or keeping for disposal or otherwise of a product directly obtained from a patented process.

2. Contributory infringement. The supply or offer to supply any of the means that relate to an essential element of the invention, for putting the invention into effect may constitute infringement. This will only be the case where there is actual or constructive knowledge that those means are suitable (and are intended) for putting the invention into effect in the UK.

Exceptions to infringement

There are a number of exceptions to patent infringement set out in the Patent Act 1977 s.60 (5)(a)-(i) the main ones being:

• Private and non-commercial use
• Experimental use

The courts have considered whether repairs to patented products constitutes infringement. The position is quite clear, genuine repair of a patented product that has been sold for use does not constitute infringement. Anyone who wishes to attack a patent by claiming for revocation can do so on the grounds that the patent is not a patentable invention 'as such' or the invention is contrary to public policy or morality, the person granted the patent is not the person entitled to the patent, the patent specification does not amount to an enabling disclosure or there has been an impermissible amendment to the patent (PA 1977 s.72).

The Intellectual Property (Unjustified Threats) Act 2017

The Intellectual Property (Unjustified Threats) Act 2017 (the "Act") received Royal Assent on 27 April 2017 and applies from 1 October 2017, making a number of amendments to the Patents Act 1977.

The Act

The Act has three key aims: (i) to protect businesses and individuals against the misuse of threats to intimidate or gain an unfair commercial advantage where there has been no infringement; (ii) to make it easier for those involved in an IP infringement dispute to negotiate a settlement, and avoid litigation; and (iii) bring consistency across the law of unjustified threats as it applied to patents, trademarks and designs.

There are a number of changes to the law surrounding unjustified threats as a result of the Act, in particular it:

- creates a new statutory test for what is a "threat of infringement proceedings";
- allows for threats to be made by "mass communication" methods;
- creates a new safe-harbour for "permitted communications";
- updates the permissible defences, to include situations in which no primary actor in an infringement can be found, despite "reasonable steps" being taken;
- creates an exception for professional advisers, under certain circumstances; and

- creates provisions for unjustified threats in relation to a unitary patent.

Threat Test

The Act modifies the "threat test", introducing an objective, two-step test to determine whether a communication amounts to a "threat of infringement proceedings". This requires that a reasonable person in the position of a recipient of the threat would understand from the communication that:

- a patent exists; and
- a person intends to enforce the patent against another person (in the UK or elsewhere) for an actual or potential infringement in the UK.

Threats need no longer be understood to relate only to bringing infringement proceedings in the UK. As a result, the provisions will apply to the unitary patent and the Act also inserts a new Schedule into the Patents Act 1977 in respect of unitary patents, for when the UPC Agreement comes into force. Furthermore, the new threat test ensures that threats to bring proceedings before the UPC in respect of patents falling within its jurisdiction will, where appropriate, fall within the scope of the threat provisions.

Who may bring an action?

It remains the law that: (i) any person "aggrieved" by a threat may bring an action; and (ii) such a threat is not actionable if it is made in respect of making or importing a product for disposal, or for using a process. In these cases, it is also not actionable to threaten proceedings for any other alleged infringement in respect of the product or process.

The Act also provides protection against threats made through mass communication, such as press releases. Such threats do not have to be directed at a particular individual.

Safe-Harbour

The Act provides a "safe harbour" to allow a patent holder to communicate with someone who might otherwise be entitled to bring an unjustified threats action if threatened. The "permitted communication" must be done for a "permitted purpose". A communication containing a threat of infringement proceedings is a "permitted communication" if:

- the communication is made solely for a "permitted purpose";
- all the information provided is necessary for that purpose; and
- the person making the communication reasonably believes it is true.

Permitted purposes include:
- notifying the recipient that the patent right exists;
- attempting to discover whether and by whom the patent is infringed (by making or importing a product, or using a process); and
- giving notice that a person has a right under a patent where that person's awareness of the patent is relevant to the action that may be taken.

The Act also grants the court the power to treat any other purpose as a "permitted purposes" if it is in the "interests of justice". The aim of this is to provide certainty over what will be considered a permitted purpose, whilst allowing the court the flexibility to take the surrounding circumstances of a case into account. The Act also lists purposes which cannot be considered "permitted purposes".

Defences and Exemptions

The old defence for making threats to secondary actors is retained, but reformed to the extent that the threatener must first use reasonable steps to discover the primary actor who is making or importing the product, or using the process. The person making the threat must also inform the person threatened either before or at the time of making the threat of the reasonable steps used.

It is also a defence to show that the act for which the threat was made is an actual or potential infringement.

Lawyers and registered patent attorneys are not liable for making threats where they have acted in their professional capacity on instructions from their client and have made that client known.

****

Ch. 3

Applying for a Patent

The pitfalls of not patenting an invention

The pitfalls of not patenting your invention are immediately obvious. If you choose not to patent your invention, anyone can use, make or sell your invention and you cannot try to stop them. You can attempt to keep your invention secret, but this may not be possible for a product where the technology is on display.

The benefits of applying for protection

Most importantly, a patent gives you the ability to take legal action to try to stop others from copying, manufacturing, selling, and importing your invention without your permission. The existence of your patent may be enough on its own to stop others from trying to exploit your invention. If it does not, the patent gives you the right to take a legal action under civil law to try to stop them exploiting your invention.

How much does it cost?

Most people are put off the idea of applying for a patent because of the cost, or potential cost. If you use a patent attorney then for sure you will pay a lot of money. However, it is relatively inexpensive to apply yourself. The IPO is taking into account the effects of COVID 19 and the delays caused when adminsitering Patents.

As stated, If you decide to seek professional IP advice (from a Patent Attorney or other representative) you will need to factor in the cost of this as well. If the patent is granted, you must pay a renewal fee to renew it every year after the 5th year for up to 20 years protection. Renewal fees start at £70 for the 5th year and rise to £610 for the 20th year.

Stage	Apply online	Apply by post
Application (if you pay when you apply)	£60	£90
Application (if you pay later-before March 31st 2021)	£60	£90
Application (if you pay later-after March 31st 2021)	£75	£112.50
Search	£150 (plus £20 for each claim over £25 claims)	£180 (plus £20 for each claim over 25 claims)
Substantive examination	£100 (plus £10 for each page of secription over 35 pages)	£130 (plus £10 for each page of description over 35 pages)

The above fees should be double checked by visiting www.gov.uk/patent-your-invention/apply-for-a-patent.

How to pay

If you apply on-line, you can pay by credit or debit card, or by deduction from your deposit account (if you have one-see below) with the IPO.

If you apply by post, you can also pay by cheque or bank transfer, but you must also fill in and send a Form FS2 fee sheet with your application. See the IPO website for further details of paying by transfer.

Deposit account

If you regularly do business with the IPO, you can pay by deposit account. This is particularly useful if you have to meet any last-minute payment deadlines.

After you apply

After you apply, the IPO will:

- check your application meets their requirements
- send you a receipt with your application number and filing date, this is the date they receive your application
- tell you what you need to do and when.

You must send claims, abstract, application fee and search fee within 12 months of your filing date, or priority date.

Request search

You must request a search within 12 months of your filing or priority date.

The IPO will check your application against published patents and documents to check your invention is new and inventive.

Publishing an application

If your application meets their requirements, they publish it just after 18 months from your filing or priority date. They will also make many documents on the open part of the file for the patent available to the public including by putting them on their website.

Your name and address will appear on the front page of the published application. Upon publication these details will also appear in IPO records and in their online Patents Journal, both of which are available to the public on their website and can be permanently searched using most standard search engines. If you do not want your home address published, you should give a different address where you can be contacted, such as a business address or a PO Box address.

Request substantive examination

You must request substantive examination within 6 months of publication. The IPO will examine your application and tell you if it meets the legal requirements. If it does not they will tell you what you need to do and how long you have to do it. This can continue for up to 4½ years from your filing or priority date.

Accelerated procedure

Various methods of accelerating the examination procedure are available - see the IPO patents fast grant guidance for further details. For example, if your application relates to an invention with an environmental benefit, accelerated processing is available through the Green Channel for patent applications. Acceleration options are also provided by the Patent Prosecution Highway and PCT (UK) Fast Track, each of which allow intellectual property offices to make use of work already conducted at another office.

Granting a patent

If your application meets the strict legal and technical requirements, the IPO will grant your patent, publish it in its final form and send you a certificate. You then need to pay renewal fees each year to keep the patent in force.

A typical patent application takes 3 to 4 years to grant, however the procedure may be accelerated as explained above. There is generally a time limit of 4½ years from the application's earliest date.

You must meet requirements within the given time limits, or your application may be terminated. However, you can extend some time limits.

If your invention is pharmaceutical or a plant protection product, you may be able to extend your patent protection with a supplementary protection certificate (SPC).

It is important to note that certain key changes to the rules governing the granting of patents came into force on October 1st 2016 and also came into force on April 1st 2017, as below.

Changes from 1 October 2016

Notification of intention to grant

On 1 October 2016, the Intellectual Property Office (IPO) started to issue a new notification of intention to grant. This letter will inform a patent applicant that their application meets all the requirements for grant of a patent. It will also state that the patent application will be sent for grant on or after a certain date. No further action will be required from the applicant in relation to the patent application in question. However, the letter will provide applicants with a clear picture of the time left to take any other action they wish before grant. In particular, there will be a clear timeframe within which to file any divisional patent application.

Simplifying the time period for requesting reinstatement

Where a patent application is terminated because the applicant unintentionally failed to meet a deadline, it is possible to request reinstatement of the application. However the current deadline for requesting reinstatement is complicated to calculate and causes confusion. The deadline changed on 1 October 2016. Applicants have 12 months from termination of their patent application to request reinstatement. The new rule is applicable to all terminated patent applications from 1 October 2016 onwards. This means that, from 1 October 2016, reinstatement may be requested in relation to any patent applications that have previously been terminated as long as no more than 12 months has passed since the date of termination. It will remain possible for the IPO to impose third-party terms when reinstating a patent application. These allow anyone who has proceeded to make or use the invention, on the basis of the application being terminated, to continue to do so.

Relaxing the requirements for formal drawings

On 1 October 2016 the legislative requirements relating to technical drawings included in patent applications were relaxed. They allow shading in drawings, providing the shading does not obscure other parts of the drawing. It will also be possible to include black and white photographs, providing they are clear and capable of reproduction. This brought the legislation more clearly into line with current IPO practice, providing clarity and legal certainty for patent applicants. The IPO will continue to reject drawings and photographs if they are not suitable for publication.

Amending international patent applications upon entry to the UK national phase

International patent applications are initially processed by the World Intellectual Property Organisation (WIPO) under the Patent Cooperation Treaty (PCT). The applicant can then choose to continue the patent application process in individual jurisdictions. This part of the process is known as the "national phase". In the UK national phase, applicants can amend their patent application voluntarily in response to reports made by the international authorities. This deals efficiently with issues raised by the international authorities, speeding up the application process as a result.

The change on 1 October 2016 will clarify when an applicant can amend their international patent application which enters the UK national phase. The first scenario is where an international search report (ISR) has been issued by the time the application enters the UK national phase. Here, the applicant can amend voluntarily from the time of UK national phase entry up until the first UK examination report is issued. The second scenario is where no ISR has been issued by the time the application enters the UK national phase. Here, the applicant can amend voluntarily from the date of issue of the UK search report or the ISR (whichever is first). Again, the cut-off is the date of issue of the first UK examination report. This rule change will bring the legislation more clearly into line with current IPO practice. It will also provide clarity and legal certainty for patent applicants. It will remain possible to amend all patent applications voluntarily in response to the first examination report, and at other times with the IPO's permission.

Clarifying requirements concerning changes of names and addresses

This change concerns name or address details registered with the IPO in relation to a patent application or a patent. The law is currently unclear about what requirements apply when a customer wishes to update this information. Such an update will be necessary when the information was previously correct but there is then a change in situation. An example may be a house move or a change of name. The legislation is being clarified to make clear that the procedure relating to corrections of names and addresses (used when there was an error in the information recorded) also applies where there has been a change in circumstances. Patents Form 20 will continue to be the form which is used to correct or update a name or address. The form was revised on 1 October 2016 to include a new tick box. This will allow the user to specify whether they wish to correct an error or to update information held by the IPO.

Advertising amendments made during proceedings

This change concerns the situation where the validity of a granted patent is challenged during infringement or revocation proceedings. The patent proprietor may request to amend the patent in order to avoid revocation. The legislation was clarified on 1 October 2016 to reflect that, under the Patents Act, the IPO has discretion over whether to advertise such amendments. In practice the only amendments not advertised would be those which are so insignificant that no-one could be expected to want to oppose them. Amendments to a patent which are proposed to avoid revocation are very unlikely to be insignificant. It follows that these amendments will be advertised. Guidance such as the

Manual of Patent Practice will set out the factors the IPO will consider before deciding whether to advertise or not.

Removing certain requirements for multiple copies of documents

From 1 October 2016 it will no longer be necessary to provide duplicate copies of Patents Form 51. This form is used to appoint or change a patent agent.

It will also no longer be necessary to file an international patent application in triplicate, when using the IPO as a receiving office under the Patent Cooperation Treaty.

Changes taking place on 6 April 2017
Allowability of omnibus claims

Patent claims define the scope of the monopoly provided by the patent by setting out the technical features present in the invention. Sometimes claims are drafted in such manner as to refer generally to the description or drawings included in the patent application. Such claims do not state the technical features of the invention claimed and are known as "omnibus claims". Understanding these claims can be difficult and can lead to a lack of clarity about the scope of protection provided by the patent. This can make it difficult for businesses to know if they are likely to infringe a competitor's patent.

From 6 April 2017 it will generally no longer be allowable to include omnibus claims in UK patent applications. They will only be allowed if the technical features of the invention cannot otherwise be clearly and concisely defined using words, a mathematical or chemical formula or any other written means. From 6 April 2017 onwards, patent examiners will raise objections to any omnibus claims present in pending patent applications. But they will not do so if the patent application has a compliance period which expires before 6 April 2017.

Furthermore, from 6 April 2017 it will no longer be possible to amend a granted patent to insert an omnibus claim. However the presence of an omnibus claim in a granted patent will not be a ground for revocation. Any granted patents including such claims will remain valid.

Limiting the use of omnibus claims will increase legal certainty for businesses looking to determine whether they can operate in a particular technology area. It will bring UK requirements into line with the requirements of the European Patent Convention (EPC) and the international Patent Cooperation Treaty (PCT). However, you should refer to the guidance on BREXIT from january 1st 2021 www.gov.uk/government/organisations/intellectual-property.

Address used to receive renewal reminders

Currently, patent holders must notify the IPO annually of the address to which renewal payment reminders are sent (where it differs from the registered address for service). From 6 April 2017, it will no longer be necessary to make this annual notification. Instead, the IPO will continue to use the address previously provided, until it is cancelled or updated by the patent holder. This change will reduce an administrative burden for patent holders. It will also provide them with an increased opportunity to use our online renewal services. These services are not available if an address is being notified at the same time as payment of the renewal fee.

*

Disputes

Hearings

Typically there are two types of dispute that you might find yourself in:

- a disagreement with the IPO regarding an objection raised against your patent application or patent, or
- a disagreement with someone else about a patent, for example an act of infringement or dispute about ownership.

If you find yourself in either of these situations, there are several ways in which the IPO can help you resolve your dispute.

Request a hearing

...to resolve a dispute between you and the Office

Sometimes, while the IPO is looking into your patent application or granted patent, they might have to object to certain things about it. You will always be given a chance to overcome these objections, but that may not always be easy. If that happens, you can ask for the matter to be referred to a senior officer at a hearing where you will be given the chance to present your arguments in person.

...to resolve a dispute between you and someone else

You may also find yourself in dispute with someone else over a patent or patent application. If this happens, the IPO might be able to help settle the dispute, but only if you refer the matter to them. If you do, then they will give both sides an opportunity to put their case to a senior officer at a hearing, often known as an "inter partes hearing". Having heard both sides of the argument, the hearing officer will issue a decision that is binding on both parties.

Alternative methods of dispute resolution

Request an opinion

If you are involved in a dispute with someone else about infringement of a patent or the validity of a patent and want to try to resolve this without getting involved in full legal proceedings you might want to consider asking the IPO for an opinion.

Mediation

Mediation is a form of alternative dispute resolution ("ADR"). It allows opposing parties to discuss the dispute with a mediator. The mediator will facilitate an exploration of the issues behind the dispute as well as any possible solutions. There are many benefits to mediation, including being able to resolve disputes spanning several countries. Mediation also offers the opportunity to explore other non-patent related disputes at the same time. To provide parties with an opportunity to mediate the IPO have set up a mediation service, details on their website.

Patent protection abroad

United Kingdom (UK) patents only give you protection in the UK, so you should consider protection abroad as well. Permission to file a patent application abroad may be required in some cases. Before considering protection abroad, ask yourself the following questions:

Do you want to sell your invention abroad?

You may not want to do this now, but you need to think ahead and decide if this is a possibility in the future.

Do you want to license your patent abroad?

This could prevent unlicensed copying or use of your invention. If you answered no to both questions, you probably do not need to apply abroad. However, please remember this allows anyone to legally make, sell or use your invention abroad. If you answered yes to either question, you should consider which option for protection abroad works best for you.

Option 1: Extend your patent

Some countries may allow you to extend your UK patent, and accept it as protected in that country after completing certain local formalities. More information about extending your UK rights abroad can be found in the Professional Section of the IPO website.

Option 2: Apply to individual national patent offices

Apply to individual national patent offices if you want protection in individual countries. You can use a certified copy to prove details about your patent when applying.

Apply under the Patent Co-operation Treaty (PCT) to countries worldwide

Apply under the European Patent Convention (EPC) to countries in Europe

Option 3: Use a combination of routes

You can use a combination of routes to apply for protection abroad. For example, you can apply in a single country, including the UK, and apply later elsewhere using the first application to claim priority.

Should you proceed with your patent application or withdraw it?

Once your patent application is published, the contents of your application and all correspondence on file will be in the public domain. It will not be possible to reverse this. Therefore you should consider carefully whether you have reasons for withdrawing the application before publication takes place. Withdrawal is the only way to prevent publication of your application, and the earlier you can notify the IPO of this, the better.

You should consider the following factors before deciding whether you want your application to be published or whether withdrawal might be a better option for you.

Why publish?

- Your application has to be published if you want a patent to be granted.

- Publication can prevent other people from patenting a similar invention, even if you choose not to proceed with our own patent application.

Why withdraw prior to publication?

- If there is information on the file for your application which you do not wish to be made public:

- All correspondence from yourself, the Office and any third parties will be open to public inspection, including on the IPO website, once your application is published. If there is information on the file which you do not want to be published, then you should withdraw your application before publication.

- This information could include sensitive information such as letters containing personal information about yourself or others, further details about your invention e.g. amended pages or claims filed after the filing date and containing additional matter, or letters giving further details explaining why your invention is different from the prior art and disclosing details.Or other information which you do not wish other people to see.

If you wish to file abroad at a later date:
You will not be able to get a patent granted in another country if the invention has already been made public. If you wish to file a patent application in another country you should therefore either do so before publication of your current application or withdraw your current application before publication.

If you wish to keep your invention secret:
You may not want other people to know what you are working on. You may decide that you want to keep the whole invention secret and rely on "trade secrets" rather than obtaining a patent.

If you have lost interest: You may decide not to pursue the patent application, through having lost interest, being unable to manufacture the invention or being unable to get financial backing.

Date of filing
The date of filing for a patent will be the date on which certain (minimum) formalities are satisfied, the rest being supplied later. The filing date is treated as the priority date. In regard to restrictions on filing abroad by UK residents, permits to first-file

abroad will need only be sought for applications relating to military technology or those prejudicial to national security or public safety.

Preliminary examination and search

The examiner will determine whether the application complies with the requirements of the Act, and then make such investigations as in his opinion are reasonably practicable and necessary for him to identify the documents needed for the substantive examination of whether the invention is new and involves an inventive step.

Publication of the application

Where the application has a date of filing it shall be published as soon as possible after the end of the prescribed period.

Substantive evaluation

The application is scrutinised to ensure that it complies with the Patents Act 1977.

Grant of patent

Where the application succeeds and the correct fee has been paid, then the Comptroller will grant the applicant a patent. The duration is 20 years from the filing date and continuation of the grant is subject to renewal fees.

The Comptroller or courts may now exercise their discretion in allowing an amendment after grant. A new section in the Patents Act 2004 (s2) requires the Comptroller and courts to have regard to any relevant principles under the European Patent Convention.

Ch. 4

Confidential Information-Breach of Confidence

This area of law has developed through the common law and equity. From the mid-nineteenth century, the law has recognised that a breach of confidence can exist and has developed since that time.

The law is aimed at protecting secrets and should not be confused with laws available in other countries providing a right to privacy. It complements other aspects of intellectual property, as an obligation of confidence can arise even before the work in question is tangible. So, for example whereas the idea for a television program cannot attract copyright protection until it is recorded in some way, the person to whom the idea is disclosed can be prevented from publicising the idea to others or by exploiting the idea by the use of an action for breach of confidence. In Fraser v Thames Television (1984) three actresses and a composer devised an idea for a television series based on the story of three female rock singers who formed a band. They discussed the idea with Thames Television and offered Thames first option on the idea, subject to the three actresses being given the parts of three rock singers.

A dispute arose, and Thames made the program without engaging the actresses. The claimants claimed breach of confidence, with the defendants arguing that the idea disclosed was not entitled to protection unless it was a developed idea that had been recorded in some permanent form. The court did not agree-those requirements were more relevant to the issue of copyright protection-and accepted the claimants argument of breach of confidence. The judge did state that to be capable of protection by the law of confidence an idea must be 'sufficiently developed, so that it would be seen to be a concept which is capable of being realised as an actuality'.

The law of breach of confidence also protects an applicant for a patent by allowing him/her to impose an obligation of confidence on those who are in a position to know, or need to know, the details of the invention before a patent application is filed. This is important because if the details of an invention are made public before the patent application is made, as we have seen, it could fail for lack of novelty. Section 2 (4)(b) of the Patents Act 1977 states that publication made in breach of confidence will not invalidate the patent application.

The conditions for imposing an obligation of confidence were stated in Megarry J's decision in Coco v A.N. Clark (Eng) Ltd (1969). The claimant who had designed an engine for a moped entered into negotiations with the defendant company to discuss manufacture of the engine. All the details of the design were disclosed during these discussions. The parties subsequently fell out and the defendant decided to make its own engine, which closely resembled the claimant's. The claimant failed in his attempt to obtain an injunction to stop the defendant manufacturing the engine. Instead the court required the defendant to deposit royalties on sales of the engines into a joint account until the full hearing. According to the judge, to be able to claim breach of confidence, a claimant needed to satisfy three conditions. First, the information must have the necessary quality of confidence. Second, the information must have been imparted in circumstances importing an obligation of confidence. Third, there must be the authorised use of information. In the case described the court felt that only the second condition could be satisfied.

Another key case was that of Michael Douglas v Hello! Magazine (No6) (2006) which concerned whether unauthorised photographs were taken in breach of confidence. The facts were that a photographer, despite heavy security, surreptitiously took photographs of a celebrity wedding. The photographs were published in the magazine *Hello!* and the celebrities sued the magazine for breach of confidence.

The main legal principle was that making it clear that photographs should not be taken, together with strict security measures, can give rise to a duty of confidence.

Each condition now needs to be considered.

The necessary quality of confidence

The first condition is that the information must have the necessary quality of confidence. In other words, it should not be in the public domain. In a commercial or industrial context this might be a trade secret. A trade secret will cover technical information, like the mechanics of an invention that is yet to be the subject of a patent application. If the information is so detailed that it cannot be carried in the head then it is a trade secret, but if it is simply a general method or scheme that is easily remembered then it is not. Even where the information is not a trade secret, it can be classified as information of a confidential nature, if it has 'the necessary quality of confidence about it, namely it must not be something which is public property and public knowledge' (Lord Greene in Saltman Engineering Co v Campbell Engineering Co (1963).

The important point is that the owner of the information has not placed it in the public domain. Confidential information can come into the public domain in a number of ways, including by applying for a patent. When a patent is applied for, details of the patent application are published on the Patents Register.

Disclosure and the 'springboard doctrine'

General disclosure or publication of information will generally remove the obligation of confidence, a person who is under an obligation of confidence may be held under that obligation for a period. This is referred to as the Springboard doctrine. One famous case here was Terrapin Ltd v Builders Supply Company (1967), the defendants made prefabricated portable buildings designed by the claimant. During the period of the agreement the claimant disclosed details of the design to the defendants in confidence. After the agreement ended the defendants produced their own buildings, which were similar to those produced by the claimant and the claimant claimed breach of confidence. Although the public could inspect the buildings at any time it was held that the defendant had acted in breach of confidence in that they should have not used information given in confidence.

Apart from the springboard doctrine, it is important to consider exactly what is confidential and what is not. Essentially, notwithstanding the above, once information is released to the public then it is not confidential. For example, several rock stars and musicians, such as Tom Jones in Woodward v Hutchins (1977) were unable to stop the publication of details of their extra marital activities because they took place in public areas and were well known.

However, just because a secret is disclosed to another person that does not necessarily place it in the public domain. One case that illustrated this is Stephens v Avery (1988) where the claimant confided to a friend that she had been involved in a lesbian relationship with the deceased wife of a known criminal. The so-called friend disclosed the information to a Sunday newspaper, claiming that the disclosure to her meant that the information ceased to be confidential. The judge, Sir Nicholas Browne-Wilkinson held that:

'The mere fact that two people know a secret does not mean that it is not confidential. If, in fact, information is secret, then in my judgement it is capable of being kept secret by the imposition of a duty of confidence on any person to whom it is communicated. Information only ceases to be confidential when it is known to a substantial number of people'.

It is clear that if a person is told something as a secret then they are under an obligation to keep that information confidential until it is clearly in the public domain.

The obligation of confidence

A second condition that arose out of Coco v Clark is that the information must have been 'imparted in circumstances importing an obligation of confidence'. In this case it is important to look at the relationship between the person imparting the information and the person who receives it. The relationship can be based on contract, trust, friendship or also marriage.

In contractual agreements the parties may have confidentiality clauses in their contracts Even if there are no express terms the parties to the contract may be under an obligation of confidence which is implied. Pre-contractual disclosures can also be binding even if no contract materialises. One such case highlights this and that is Tournier v National Provincial and Union Bank of England (1924), it was held that the bank was under an obligation of confidence to its customers, unless required to disclose information by law.

Contracts of employment impose or imply quite clear duties of confidence. However, importantly, there is no duty to keep a secret about an employer's wrongful or unlawful acts. The obligation of confidence can continue even after the contract of employment has come to an end. One important case highlighting this was Faccenda Chicken Ltd v Fowler (1986) the claimant who sold fresh chickens from refrigerated vans, applied for an injunction to prevent two former employees from using their knowledge of sales, prices and customers details, when they set up a competing business. The judge said that in deciding whether the former employees owed a duty of confidence in respect of this information a number of factors should be considered:

- the nature of the employment. Was confidential information habitually, normally or only occasionally handled by the employer?

- The nature of the information itself: only trade secrets or information of a highly confidential nature would be protected.

- Whether the employer impressed upon the employee the confidential nature of the information.

- Whether the relevant information could be isolated easily from other information that the employee was free to use or disclose.

While one of the employees in question was employed there was information that could be regarded as confidential and could not be disclosed by him, or used for any other purpose as it was in breach of contract. However, when the contract of employment ended, such information that had become part of his own skill and knowledge ceased to be confidential and the employee was entitled to make use of that information and those skills. Independent contractors, while not under a contract of employment, are usually under a duty of confidence by virtue of terms expressed or implied by law in a contract for services.

Non-contractual relationships

The obligation of confidence is not restricted to contractual relationships. For example it can apply between doctor and patient, subject to public interest defence. A secret between friends can give rise to an obligation of trust.

This was highlighted in Stephens v Avery, as described. What ties the different relationships together is that, as stated in Coco v Clark by J Megarry:

'The circumstances are such that any reasonable man standing in the shoes of the recipient of the information would have realised that upon reasonable grounds the information was given him in confidence'.

Another test was applied in Carflow Products (UK) Ltd v Linwood Securites (Birmingham) Ltd (1966) where the judge use a subjective test, i.e. what obligations did the parties intend to impose and accept? In that case, because both parties wanted to invalidate a third party's registered design right by showing that it had been previously been available in the public domain, both party's agreed that they did not intend the information to be treated as confidential. The judge also imposed an objective test that could be used if the subjective test was not answered. This test was the same as that used in the Coco v Clark case.

The obligation of trust will extend to third parties if it is obvious that the information is of a confidential nature. For example, as in cases such as Stephens and Avery. The media is under an obligation not to publish information of a confidential nature passed on by a recipient. In the same way, where an ex-employee is under an obligation of confidence the new employer will be too.

Unauthorised use of information

Megarry J's third condition in Coco v Clark was that the information has been used without the owner's authority. Within an agreement involving obligations of confidence, there will be implied as well as express terms. It will be clear that certain information is confidential. However, it may be necessary to disclose the information to others not directly party to the agreement. For example, where one party is engaged to manufacture the subject of the agreement, employees on the shop floor will need to have access to the information covered by the agreement in order to produce the end product, as well as sub-contractors. The authority to disclose in this instance will be implied into the agreement, even if not expressly contained.

One other question to be asked is, can a co-owner of information prevent its use by other co-owners?

In Drummond Murray v Yorkshire Fund Managers Ltd and Michael Hartley (1998) this was clearly illustrated. The claimant was a marketing expert involved in the purchase of companies. He joined a team of five for the purpose of management buy out/in of a company. The group created a business plan to interest venture capitalists. The business plan and the price to be paid for assets were highly confidential. Each member of the group was a co-author of the business plan with equal rights in it. However, there was no agreement between group members as to how this confidential information should be used.

The group approached the defendants as potential investors. The business plan and the price to be paid for the assets were discussed. The first defendant was interested in investing in the company but questioned the claimant's involvement as managing director and the group, other than the claimant, agreed for the latter to be replaced by the second defendant. The claimant sued for breach of confidential information, contending that the confidential information was given to the defendants for the purpose of deciding whether to invest. The second defendant was therefore not entitled to use that information for any other purpose and had breached this obligation by using this information for the purpose of replacing him as managing director.

The Court of Appeal held that the confidential information was incidental to the relationship between the group members. The confidential information ceased to be the claimant's property once this information was dissolved. As there had been no agreement between group members the claimant could not prolong that relationship once he ceased to be a group member.

Defences

Confidential information and the public interest

The only real defence to this form of action is that disclosure of the information is in the public interest. As with copyright, the law of confidence is not available to protect confidential information that is considered immoral. The Human Rights Act 1998 has accorded a greater significance to the public interest defence, especially to the statutory recognition that it offers to the right to privacy and the freedom of expression.

Remedies

Damages for breach of confidence will generally be calculated on the basis of compensating the claimant for the conversion of property. There are many ways to arrive at a sum for compensation and this will depend on the individuals case and loss incurred. The Court of Appeal, in Indata Equipment Supplies Ltd v ACL Ltd (1998) stated that damages should be assessed on a tortious basis, that is such sum as would put the claimant into the position he would have been had it not been for the tort, or breach of confidence.

As with infringement of other intellectual property rights, the claimant can request an account of profits where the information has been used commercially. This is an equitable remedy that is at the courts discretion, as is an order for the delivery up and destruction of goods made using the confidential information.

As this area of law is concerned with confidential information, the usual remedy sought is that of an injunction preventing disclosure of information, if this is practical and the information is not already in the public domain.

Ch. 5

Trade Marks and the Law

Definition of a trademark and historical background

A trademark is a symbol or a sign placed on, or used in relation to, one trader's goods or services to distinguish them from similar goods or services supplied by other traders. Section 1 of the Trade Marks Act 1994, as amended, which is the main legislation covering trade marks, defines a trade mark as any sign capable of being represented graphically which distinguishes the goods or services of one business from those of another.

The enactment of the 1994 Act radically changed the law dealing with registered trademarks. The legislation harmonises the trade mark law of the United Kingdom with that of the rest of the European Community and implements the first council directive (89/104/EEC) to approximate the laws of the member states relating to trademarks. The Government also took the opportunity with the 1994 Act to bring the law up to date, as the previous Act, the 1938 Act was inadequate in its scope and coverage.

From 14 January 2019 the long-awaited Trade Mark Directive (2015/2436) and implemented into Law via the Trade Marks Regulations 2018, took effect in the UK, reflecting the UK's continued effort to enhance harmonisation of trade mark law across the EU. This is described in more detail later in the chapter, and also in the chapter on trademark applications.

Brexit & Trade Marks

International trade mark registrations protected in the EU under the Madrid Protocol will no longer enjoy protection in the UK after 1 January 2021.

Of all the intellectual property rights, trade mark practice is likely to be the most impacted by Britain's leaving the EU. The UK's existing trade mark law is heavily entwined with EU law – in particular via the EU Trade Mark Directive. Domestic UK trade marks will be unaffected. EU Trade Marks (EUTMs) on the other hand are registered with the EU Intellectual Property Office. Many companies have relied upon EUTMs rather than national trade mark registrations for their trade mark protection in Europe. The consequences of the UK ceasing to be an EU Member State are therefore of great importance.

What will happen to EUTM's once the UK leaves the EU?

The Withdrawal Agreement has a section devoted to intellectual property rights. Holders of EUTMs that have been registered before the end of the transition period will automatically be granted a comparable UK trade mark, for the same sign and covering the same goods and services. The filing date of the comparable UK trade mark will be the same as that of the EUTM on which it is based. Where applicable, the comparable UK trade mark will also enjoy the seniority of any relevant UK trade mark.

This does not address the situation where an EUTM has been applied for but not granted by the end of the transition period. For new trade mark filings it may therefore be prudent, where the UK is of any significance as a territory as well as EU27 countries, to file for both UK national and EU trade mark protection, in particular, if the application was made towards the end of the transition period. Alternatively, there will be a period of 9 months following the end of the transition period in which it will be possible to file a UK trade mark application and claim the filing date of an identical EUTM application that was still pending at the end of the transition period.

Will a trade mark attorney still be able to manage my portfolio post-Brexit?

For firms with attorneys based solely in the UK, the position is less clear, as the EU has indicated that, following the transition period, UK-based trade mark attorneys may lose representation rights before the EUIPO. Ultimately, the regulatory position regarding professional representatives for EU trade marks will depend on the final trading terms agreed upon between the UK and the EU.

For on-going matters, the Withdrawal Agreement stipulates that those authorised to appear before the EUIPO and currently representing a client in a 'procedure' before the end of the transition period will be able to continue representing their client in that procedure.

Historical background

Traders have, from the earliest times, distinguished their goods by marking them. By the 19th century it had become very clear that marks applied to goods that had become distinctive had an intrinsic value and needed some form of legal protection lacking at the time. Such protection was available through the use of Royal Charters and court action, which involved injunctions or action for infringement, although clearly this was not adequate or far reaching enough.

The Trademark Registration Act 1875 was passed to overcome the difficulties encountered in court actions. The Act established a statutory Register of Trademarks that is still in use today. The Register provides the trademark owner with proof of title to, and exclusive rights of use of, the trademark for the goods in respect of which it is registered. The Act of 1875 also laid down the essentials of a trademark. A number of Acts followed, the Patents, Designs and Trademarks Act 1883, the Trademarks Act 1905 and the Trademarks Act 1919. These Acts culminated in the 1938 Trademarks Act which in turn was replaced by the 1994 Trademarks Act.

International Provisions

There are a number of international conventions and arrangements that give some international recognition to national trademarks. These are the Paris Convention, The Madrid Arrangement and the Protocol to the Madrid arrangement (Madrid Protocol). There is also a Community Trademarks System that creates a trademark that gives rights throughout the European Community and which will be referred to below.

Paris Convention

The Paris Convention came into being in 1883. Its overall purpose was to create recognition between various countries of each other's national intellectual property rights, through the concept of priority.

Priority recognises the first filing date for a particular intellectual property right in any convention country as the filing date for all other convention countries in respect of the same property right. The period of priority differs from intellectual property right to intellectual property right but for trademarks the period is six months. This has given a level of international protection for trade marks because the first to file a trade mark application is, in most countries, the person with better claim to a trade mark.

In England, this is not the case because rights in passing off (see later) can be built up through sufficient use of a trademark, without registration, and these rights can act as an obstacle to any subsequent application to register the trademark by a third party.

Another provision of the Paris Convention relevant to trade marks is Article 6, which gives international protection to 'well known' trademarks. A person can own a well-known trademark in registered or unregistered form even in countries where the action of passing off does not exist. Ownership of a well known mark will prevent a third party from applying to register the same or similar mark in any other convention country that has implemented Article 6 and allows cancellation of an existing registration for such an identical or similar mark during the first five years after registration on the application of the owner of the well known mark.

The Madrid Agreement

The Madrid Agreement was implemented in 1891 to simplify the procedure for filing trademark registration in many countries. The Madrid Agreement aimed to replace the multiple filing of trademark registrations in (10) individual countries.

The Madrid Agreement allows anyone established or domiciled in an Agreement country, with a trademark registration in his or her country, to file one international application that will cover all Madrid Agreement countries. The central application is filed with the offices of the World Intellectual Property Rights Organisation (WIPO) in Geneva. This is then administered by that office. England did not sign the Madrid Agreement so this is not available to English trademark owners.

The Madrid Protocol

As a number of key countries did not sign the Madrid Agreement, discussions began in the mid-1980's on how to make the Madrid system more palatable. The result was the Madrid Protocol established in 1989. At the current time there are 42 signatories to the protocol including the UK. Up to date information concerning the countries and the protocol see www. ltma.org.uk

The protocol is based on essentially the same structure as the Madrid Agreement, with a few differences designed to allow more flexibility.

Although classed as an international registration system, the CTM operates differently from either the Madrid Agreement or Madrid Protocol. It is more like the national system (see below) in that it is a means of filing an application for one trade mark at one trade mark registry to obtain one registration under one set of laws and procedures. The only difference is that the area covered by the registration is a collection of countries within the European Union.

The application can be filed in The CTM Office in Alicante Spain or at the National Trademark office in any member country, which passes the application to the CTO Office.

Trademarks and registration of trademarks

As discussed, the function of a trademark is to distinguish between one trader's goods and another trader's goods. The function of an ordinary trade mark is to act as an indicator of trade origin, which aids both consumers of branded goods and the trade mark proprietor, as follows:

1) The trademark acts as an indicator of quality and reliability, protecting consumers from confusion or deception in the market place.
2) The trademark can be enforced to protect the mark's proprietor against certain acts of unfair competition.

Collective marks and certification marks

Although they are rare, such trademarks perform different functions compared to ordinary trademarks. Certification marks (Trademarks Act 1994 s.50) are intended to indicate that goods or services comply with a certain objective standard as to quality, origin, material, the mode of manufacture of goods or the performance of services or other characteristics. Any third party whose goods or services meet the required standards may apply to be an authorised user of a certification mark and the proprietor cannot refuse this request.

Collective marks serve to indicate members of an association. A third party who is not a member of that association does not have the right to use the mark. Collective marks can act as certification marks and vice versa.

Trademark law

As seen, in the UK, trademarks are governed by the 1994 Trademarks Act, as amended by the below:

The Trade Marks (EC Measures Relating to Counterfeit Goods) Regulations 1995 (SI 1995/1444) *(1 July 1995)*;

Section 13 of the Olympic Symbol etc (Protection) Act 1995 *(21 September 1995)*;

Part IV of the Patents and Trade Marks (World Trade Organisation)

Regulations 1999 (SI 1999/1899) *(29 July 1999)*;

Section 6 of the Copyright, etc. and TradeMarks (Offences and Enforcement) Act 2002 *(20 November 2002)*;

The TradeMarks (Proof of Use, etc.) Regulations 2004 (SI 2004/946) *(5*

May 2004); $ the Trade Marks (International Registrations Designating

the European Community, etc.) Regulations 2004 (SI 2004/2332) *(1*

October 2004);

The Serious Organised Crime and Police Act 2005 (*19 April 2005*); and

The Intellectual Property (Enforcement, etc.) Regulations 2006 (SI

2006/1028) *(29 April 2006)*.

The Legal Services Act 2007

The Trade Marks (Relative Grounds) Order 2007

The TradeMarks (Earlier Trade Marks) Regulations 2008 (SI 2008/1067) (10 May 2008)

The Trade Mark Directive (2015/2436) effective from 14th January 2019)

European Withdrawal Acts 2018/ 2020 and associated Regulations

An application for a national trademark may be made to the Intellectual Property Office (see next chapter). As we have discussed, as a consequence of Brexit, which became effective on December 31st, 2020, trademarks registered in the European Community, international trademark registrations designated by the European Union Intellectual Property Office (EUIPO) and Community designs, ceased to have effect in the United Kingdom as of January 1st, 2021, keeping their validity in the other 27 member countries of the European Union (EU).

Notwithstanding the foregoing, designs and Community trademarks registered with the EUIPO before December 31st, 2020, shall be automatically cloned in the United Kingdom and assigned a new registration number at the national level, which shall grant their holders the same rights as the pre-existing registrations in the United Kingdom. All dates of the original registration shall be maintained, such as, filing dates, priority and seniority.

Not all marks are capable of being registered as trademarks. Objections to the registration of a mark may be raised, either by the IPO during examination of the mark or by third parties during any opposition actions or proceedings. The grounds for refusing registration are divided into two categories:

1. Absolute grounds for refusal (TMA 1994 s.3 and 4) which are concerned with objections based on the mark itself.
2. Relative grounds for refusal (TMA 1994 s.5) these being concerned with a conflict and third party rights.

Classification of a trade mark
The Nice Agreement for the International Classification of Goods and Services provides that there are thirty-four classes of goods and eight classes of services. Any application for registration

must stipulate which classes, or sub-classes, in which registration is sought. Multi-class applications are possible and it would, in theory, be possible to register a mark in respect of all forty two classes. However, this is very unlikely as applicants must have a bona fide intent to use the marks for the prescribed goods and services (TMA 1994 ss.3 (6) and 32 (3)).

Limited registration for retail service marks is also now possible in class 35. This change follows OHIM's decision in Giacomelli Sports Spa (1999).

Definition of a trade mark

The 1994 Trademarks Act s.1(1) provides that a trade mark is a sign capable of being represented graphically, capable of distinguishing goods or services of one undertaking, from those of another undertaking. There are a number of elements in the definition:

a) *A 'sign'*. The concept of a sign in UK trademark law is very broad indeed. Although there is no clear definition, signs provided in the UK include works, designs and shapes and also more unconventional marks such as sounds and smells. A sign can be regarded as anything that conveys information (Phillips v Remington (1998) See below.

b) *Graphic representation*. Signs must be represented graphically, i.e. be represented in such a way that third parties may determine and understand what the sign is,. This requirement is normally satisfied by including an image of the mark in the trade mark application. However, it has been suggested that provision of an image is not absolutely necessary provided that third parties can clearly identify the mark from the description (Swizzels Matlow Ltds Application

(1999). It may be difficult to graphically represent unconventional marks, but practice dictates for example that sound marks are represented by music notation and that for shape marks it is best to submit line drawings or photographs. Applications for colour marks will usually include a representation of the colour and so on.

c) *Capable of distinguishing.* Signs must be capable of distinguishing goods or services of one undertaking from another undertaking. Any sign that has the capacity to distinguish will satisfy this requirement.

Absolute grounds for refusal

The main legislation is Section 3(1)(a-d) Trade Marks Act 1994, Art 3 (1) (a-d) Directive on the Legal protection of Trade marks. A sign will not be registered if it falls within one or more of the absolute grounds for refusing registration.

Signs not satisfying the s.1 (1) requirements

Signs which do not meet the definition of 'trade mark' provided in the Trademarks act 1994 will not be registered. In addition, it is important for an applicant not to make a mistake as to the graphic representation as the opportunities to correct or amend are very limited (TMA 1994 s.39 prevents the correction of errors in a trade mark application that would substantially affect the identity of the trade mark). This is mitigated by the fact that it is IPO practice to examine marks for graphic representation before a filing date is allocated.

Scent marks continue to cause considerable difficulties for graphic representation. John Lewis Application (The scent of Cinnamon) (2001) indicates a description of a scent is unlikely to be precise enough.

Signs must also be capable of distinguishing the goods or services of one undertaking form those of other undertakings. As noted above, this is not a high standard and, in effect, it will only bar those signs that are incapable of functioning as trademarks (e.g. the Philips shaver shape in Philips Electronics v Remington Consumer Products (1999) a case discussed below, was held not to be distinctive in a trade mark sense and thus did not satisfy TMA 1994, s.3 (1)(a)).

Marks devoid of distinctive character or those consisting of exclusively descriptive or generic signs are prohibited unless it can be shown that before the application was made, a mark has acquired a distinctive character as a result of a use made of it. This proviso to the TMA 1994 ss.3 (1)(b)(c) and (d) means that there is no absolute prohibition as a matter of law on non-distinctive, descriptive and generic marks. As recognised in British Sugar v James Robertson (TREAT) 1996, such marks may be registered where they have become factually distinctive upon use despite the provisions stated in the TMA 1994 s.3 (1)(b)-(d). This proviso does not apply to TMA 1994 s.3(1)(a) or any other absolute ground for refusal.

Marks devoid of distinctive character

TMA 1994 s.3 (1)(b) prevents the registration of marks that are not, prima facie, distinctive. An example might include a surname common in the UK. In British Sugar v James Robertson (TREAT) 1996, it was said that a mark is devoid of distinctive character where the sign cannot distinguish the applicants goods or services without the public being first educated that it is a trademark. The mark at issue in this case, TREAT, for a syrup for pouring on ice cream and desserts, was therefore devoid of distinctive character. Such marks may, nevertheless, benefit from the TMA 1994 s.3 (1)(b) proviso. Therefore trademarks will only fail where they are not distinctive by nature and have not become distinctive by nurture.

Signs that are exclusively descriptive

For a sign to be open to objection under TMA 1994 s.3 (1)(c) the trademark must consist exclusively of a sign which may be used in trade to describe characteristics of the goods or services. The sub-categories of TMA 1994 s.3 (1)(c) are:

1) Kind. Terms indicating kind or type that should be free for all traders to use, e.g. PERSONAL for computers, are not normally registrable.
2) Quality. Laudatory words, e.g. PERFECTION, are not usually registrable.
3) Quantity. The Trade Marks Registry gives the example that 454 would not be registrable for butter, as butter is frequently sold for domestic consumption in 454g (1lb) packs. Where numerical marks are not descriptive or otherwise objectionable, they may be registered.
4) Intended purpose. Generally, words referring to the purpose of goods or services are not registrable.
5) Value. Signs pertaining to the value of goods or services are not normally registrable, e.g. BUY ONE GET TWO FREE.
6) Geographical origin. Geographical names are not usually registrable unless used in specific circumstances.
7) Time of production of goods or the rendering of services. Typically, marks such as SAME DAY DELIVERY for courier services or AUTUMN 2004 for haute couture would not be registrable.

8) Other characteristics of goods and services. For example, a representation of the good or service would not usually be registrable.

Marks falling into any of these categories may still be registrable if they have become distinctive upon use.

Signs that are exclusively generic

TMA 1994 s.3(1)(d) prohibits the registration of signs or indications that have become customary in the current language or in the bone fide and established practices of the trade. An example can be found in JERYL LYNN Trademark (1999) where an application for JERYL LYNN for vaccines was refused as the mark described a strain of vaccine and was not distinctive of the applicant.

Shapes that cannot be registered

Traditionally in the UK, shapes were not registrable. One case highlighting this was Coca-Cola's trademark application (1986).

However, the TMA 1994 makes it very clear that the shapes of goods and their packaging are now registrable (TMA 1994 s.1 (1)), but the TMA 1994 s.3 (2) excludes certain shapes from registration. This is an area of trademark law that has lacked clarity.

ECJ guidance on the registrability of shape marks has clarified matters somewhat. The UK Court of Appeal stayed proceedings in Phillips Electronics v Remington Consumer products (1999) to allow a preliminary reference to the ECJ in a number of issues, including questions specific to shape marks and this decision has implications for the interpretation of the TMA 1994 s.3 (2). In this case, Philips had been producing a three-headed rotary shaver for a considerable time (the Philishave). When Remington produced a rotary shaver of a similar design Philips sued for infringement of a mark which was the face of the three headed shaver. The TMA 1994 provides that the following shapes are not registrable:

1) Where the shape results from the nature of the goods themselves. Inherent shapes therefore cannot be registered. In the Philips case, The Court of Appeal considered that there would be no objection to Philips three headed shaver shape on this ground as electronic shavers can take other forms.

2) Where the shape of the goods is necessary to achieve a technical result (TMA 1994 s.3 (2)(b). Functional shapes are therefore not registrable. In Philips 1999 case it was considered that the shaver shape was necessary to achieve a technical result, but the ECJ was, nevertheless, asked to adjudicate in the matter, i.e. on the correct approach to functional shapes. They concurred in the matter. They also confirmed that the fact that there may be more than one shape that could achieve the same result is not relevant. Consequently, it appears that only shapes with specifically non-functional aspects are registrable.

3) Where the shapes gives substantial value to the goods. In Philips (1999) the Court of Appeal suggested that a valuable shape in this context can be identified where the shape itself adds substantial value, e.g. the shape adds value via eye appeal or functional effectiveness. In contrast, shapes that are valuable because they are 'good trademarks' would not fall foul of the TMA 1994.

Marks likely to give offence or deceive

A mark will not be registered if it is contrary to public policy or accepted principles of morality (TMA 1994 s.3 (3)(a) or is of such a nature that it is likely to deceive the public. For example, as to the nature, quality or origin of the goods or services.

Relatively few marks are deemed to be contrary to public policy or morality. Morality should be considered in the context of current thinking and only where a substantial number of persons would be offended should registration be refused.. For example, in BOCM's application, (EUROLAMB) (1997) EUROLAMB was considered to be deceptive if used in relation to non-sheep meat (when used in relation to sheep meat it was descriptive). It is very clear that the test of deception is deceptive and actual evidence of deception must be provided.

Marks prohibited by UK or EC law

The registration of marks whose use would be illegal under UK or Community law is precluded by TMA 1994 s.3(1)(d).

Protected emblems

TMA 1994 s.4 provides details of marks that are considered to fall into the category of specially protected emblems, e.g. marks with Royal connotations, and the Olympic symbol cannot be registered. Marks containing such emblems cannot be registered without consent.

Applications made in bad faith

The key statute here is Section 3(3)(a) and (b) and section 3(6) Trade Marks Act 1994, Art 3(1)(f) and (2)(d) Directive on the Legal Protection of Trade Marks:

(3) A trade mark shall not be registered if it is -

(a) contrary to public policy or accepted principles of morality, or
(b) of such a nature as to deceive the public
(6) A trade mark shall not be registered if or to the extent that the application is made in bad faith.

There is no requirement that a mark need be used prior to the application for registration, but the applicant must have a bona fide intention to use the mark and applications may be refused when they are made in bad faith. Therefore, so-called ghost applications should be caught by this section.

Relative grounds for refusal
Section 5(1) Trade Marks act 1994, Art 4(1)(a) Directive on the Legal Protection of Trade marks:
(1) A trade mark shall not be registered if it is identical with an earlier trade mark and the goods or services for which the trade mark is applied for are identical with the goods or services for which then earlier trade mark is protected.

The applicant must also overcome the relative grounds for refusing registration. These relate to conflict with earlier marks or earlier rights. The 'earlier mark' (TMA 1994 s.6) might be a trademark registered in the UK or under the Madrid Protocol. Alternatively it might be a CTM or a well-known mark (the latter are entitled to protection as per article 6 of the Paris Convention for the Protection of Industrial Property 1883).

There is no provision for honest concurrent use in the TMA 1994. As it has been made clear that a trade mark application must be refused, irrespective of honest concurrent use, if the registered proprietor objects, this provision is of limited value to the applicant. If the proprietor of the registered mark objects, honest concurrent use provides no defence.

Conflict with an earlier mark for identical goods or services
The TMA 1994 s.5 (1) only provides the narrowest relative ground for refusing registration: a mark identical to an earlier trademark and used for identical goods and services will not be registered. The requirement of 'identical goods and services' is sufficiently broad in scope to include cases where the applicants mark is identical to only some of the goods and services for which the earlier mark is registered, but to 'constitute an 'identical mark' a very high level of identity between the marks is required. One such case highlighting this is Origins Natural Resources v Origins Clothing (1995).

The registration of similar marks for the same or similar services is only prohibited where confusion on the part of the public is likely to arise (TMA 1994 s.5 (2). Specifically what is prohibited is the registration of:

1) Identical marks for similar goods or services or
2) Similar marks for identical/similar goods or services where, because of the identity or similarity, there is a likelihood of confusion on the part of the public, which includes the likelihood of association with the earlier trade mark.

What constitutes 'confusing similarity' has been considered at length by the ECJ (Sabel v Puma 1998) and Canon v Metro Goldwyn Meyer (1999). Confusion has to be appreciated globally taking into account all factors relevant to the case. These factors include:

- The recognition of the earlier trade mark on the market
- The association that can be made between the registered mark and the sign
- The degree of similarity between the mark and the sign and the goods and the services, the degree of similarity must be considered in deciding whether the similarity is sufficient so as to lead to a likelihood of confusion

It has also been made clear that 'likelihood of association' is not an alternative to 'likelihood of confusion" but serves to define its scope. This means that if the public merely makes an association between two trademarks, this would not in itself be sufficient for concluding that there would be a likelihood of confusion. There is no likelihood of confusion where the public would not believe that goods or services came from the same undertaking.

Conflict with a mark of repute

A mark that is identical or similar to an earlier mark will be refused registration in respect of dissimilar goods or services where the earlier mark is a mark of repute and the use of the later mark would, without the cause, take unfair advantage of or be detrimental to the reputed mark's distinctiveness or reputation. (TMA 1994 s5 (3).

A mark of repute is a mark with a reputation in the UK (for CTM applications it must have a reputation in the EU). In deciding as to whether a trade mark has a reputation, the ECJ has provided some guidance (General Motors Corp v Yplon) (2000). Repute would be judged with reference to the general public or to a specific section of the public, and the mark must be known to a significant portion of that public.

Relevant indicators of the public's knowledge of the mark include the extent and duration of the trade marks use, its market share and the extent to which it has been promoted.

In order for registration to be refused under s.5 (3) use of the applicants mark will have to take unfair advantage of or be detrimental to the reputed marks distinctiveness or reputation. In OASIS STORES LTD's application (EVEREADY) (1998) it was said that merely being reminded of an opponents mark did not itself amount to taking unfair advantage. The fact that the applicant did not benefit to any significant extent from their opponent's reputation and the wide divergence between the parties goods was relevant, s.5 (3) could not be intended to prevent the registration of any mark identical or similar to a mark of repute.

Conflict with earlier rights

TMA 1994 s.5 (4) provides that where a mark conflicts with earlier rights, including passing off, design rights and copyright the mark will not be registered.

Surrender, revocation, invalidity, acquiescence and rectification

Surrender. It is possible to surrender a trademark with respect to some or all of the goods or services for which it is registered. Marks may be revoked (removed from the registry on three grounds: non-use because the mark has become generic; or because the mark has become deceptive. A mark will be invalid if it breaches any of the absolute grounds for registration.

Where the proprietor of an earlier trade mark or other right is aware of the use of a mark subsequently registered in the UK and has, for a continuous period of five years, taken no action regarding that use the proprietor is said to have acquiesced. Where this is the case, the proprietor of the earlier mark or right cannot rely on his right in applying for a declaration of invalidity or in opposing the use of the later mark, unless it is being used in bad faith.

Anyone with sufficient interest can apply to rectify an error or omission in the register. Such a rectification must not relate to matters that relate to the validity of the trademark.

Infringement

Section 10(1) Trade Marks Act 1994, Art 5 (1)(a) Directive on the Legal Protection of Trade Marks:

'A person infringes a registered trade mark if he uses in the course of trade a sign which is identical with the trade mark in relation to goods or services which are identical with those for which it is registered'.

The proprietor (and any exclusive licensee) has certain rights to a mark (TMA 1994 s.9 (1) which are infringed by certain forms of unauthorised use of the mark in the UK. These rights come into existence from the date of registration, which is the date of filing. All infringement acts require the mark to be used in the UK in the course of trade. What constitutes 'use' of a mark has been the subject matter of some debate and is discussed below.

Use of an identical sign for identical goods or services

Use, in the course of trade, of an identical sign, in respect of goods or services constitutes trademark infringement (TMA 1994 s.10 (1).

Use of an identical or similar sign on identical or similar goods or services

Use, in the course of trade, of an identical sign or similar goods or services (TMA 1994 s.10 (2) (a) or a similar sign on identical goods or services constitutes infringement where the public is likely to be confused as to the origin of goods or services or is likely to assume that there is an association with the registered mark.

Use of a mark similar to a mark of repute for dissimilar goods or services

Registered marks with a 'reputation' are infringed if an identical or similar mark is used for non-similar goods or services, where the use takes unfair advantage of or is detrimental to, the distinctive character or repute of the distinctive mark (TMA 1994 s.10 (3).

Contributory infringement

TMA 1994 s.10 (5) is known as the contributory infringement provision. This provision creates a form of secondary participation where a person who applies a trademark to certain materials has actual or constructive knowledge that the use of the mark is not authorised. This provision extends infringement down the supply chain, but printers, publishers, manufacturers or packaging etc. may avoid a s. 10 (5) liability in practice by inserting suitable contractual forms into their agreement with their clients.

Defences to infringement

a) Comparative advertising. Comparative advertising is allowed under certain circumstances as long as the use is not unfair or detrimental. One such case that highlights this is British Airways PLC v Ryanair Ltd (2001). British Airways had brought an action for infringement against Ryanair for the publication of two Ryanair advertisements comparing fares with BA. The courts found that, in assessing as to whether a mark has been used in accordance with honest practice, the court should view the advertisement as a whole. Although misleading adverts cannot be honest, on the facts, whilst the advertisement at issue may have caused offence it was not dishonest and the price comparisons were not significantly unfair.

b) The use of another registered mark. The use of one registered mark, within the boundaries of the registration, does not infringe another registered mark.

c) Use of own name or address. A person using their own name or address does not infringe a registered mark, providing that the use accord with open honest practice. However, see the note on the Trade Mark Directive introduced in 2019.

d) Use of certain indications. The use of certain indications (e.g. the intended purpose of the gods or services or their geographical origin) will not constitute infringement where that use accords with appropriate honest practice.

e) The locality defence. Signs applicable to a certain locality whose use predates the registration of a mark may continue to be used in that locality.

f) Exhaustion. Trademark rights are exhausted once the proprietor has consented to the placing of goods bearing the mark on the market within the EEA. For example, once a brand owner consents to a consignment of their goods being marketed in France, trademark rights cannot be used to prevent these goods from being resold in the UK, unless there are legitimate reasons for this. Goods sold in this way are known as 'grey imports' or parallel imports.

Please note that the Trade Mark Directive (2015/2436) introduced from 14th January 2019, and implemented into Law via the Trade Marks Regulations 2018, makes the following changes to infringement defences:

a. Own-name defence: the use of a trade mark as (or part of) a company name may now be found to be an infringing act. This defence now only applies if you are using your own personal name.

b. Non-use defence: As part of your defence during proceedings, you can now ask the owners of the registered mark to show that their mark is valid i.e. that they have been using it. This is easier than commencing parallel revocation proceedings based upon a claim of non-use.

c. If you applied to registered/started to use a mark that was similar/identical to an earlier registered once that mark had expired and then the owner of the earlier mark renews/restores it, they may now claim you are infringing this registration. Under certain circumstances, you may have a defence against such a claim.

In relation to invalidation proceedings, new amendments mean that the claimant may have to demonstrate more substantial evidence that their earlier rights are valid.

You should note that the Trade Mark Directive (2015/2346) introduced in january 2019, and implemented into Law via the

Trade Marks Regulations 2018, has introduced the following changes in respect of Trade Mark disputes:

1. In the event that you think fake or counterfeit goods under your mark are passing through the UK enroute to countries outside the customs territory of the EU, you can request that the customs authorities detain them. In any such dispute, it will now be up to the person shipping the goods to prove that you have no right to stop them being marketed in the destination country. (it is no longer required that the trade mark owner prove that the goods coming from the outside of the EU were intended to be put on sale in the UK). The burden of proof has now shifted to the importer.

2. Further to the above, a more extensive range of (counterfeit) activities will be treated as infringement. This should make it more difficult for parties that contribute to counterfeiting to avoid prosecution.

3. As the registered trade mark owner, you can now take action against publishers who have incorrectly identified your trade mark as a generic term in a dictionary etc. You may now ask the publisher to make it clear that the mark is registered, and if they fail to do so you can apply to the court to order that the publisher correct the entry or amend the entry, destroy copies of the publication, or order other remedies, as appropriate.

4. If someone acting as your trade mark agent or representative has applied for or registered your trade mark without your permission there are now provisions in place for you to rectify the ownership on the Register as well as to invalidate the registration.

5. Prior to 14 January 2019, it was not possible to bring infringement proceedings against another registered mark unless you had firstly invalidated it. Now, the courts will consider invalidation-related issues during the course of infringement proceedings. Importantly, the courts will take into consideration the length of time you knew that the other was being genuinely used before taking legal action.

In addition to the above, the Directive has also introduced the following changes, which are als relevant to the next chapter:

If you licence use of your trade mark, it is now possible for you (as the trade mark owner) to take legal action under UK trade mark law, (as opposed to contract law) against the licensee if they fail to observe correctly the provisions in the licence which deal with how long the agreement lasts, what goods/services the licence covers, geographic area the mark can be used and quality etc.

Where previously, you were able to divide your application, it is now possible to divide registrations in the event of a dispute.

From 14 January 2019, the UK IPO will send out renewal reminders about 6 months before the renewal fee is due to be paid and your registration expires. Reminders were previously sent out about 4 months before the due date.

If you fail to renew your trade mark registration and you wish to 'restore' it, the UK IPO will now assess whether the registration should be restored based on whether the failure to renew was 'unintentional' (previously the test had been whether it was 'just' to renew your mark). The IPO will no longer have to consider other marks when deciding whether to restore your mark.

Ch. 6

Applying for a Trade Mark-The Practical Process

Before discussing the actual proces of application, note that, as mentioned in the previous chapter, from the 14th of January 2019 the EU Trade Mark Directive 205/2436 took effect in the UK (implemented into Law via the Trade Marks Regulations 2018), which introduced the following changes to the application process:

1. When filing a UK TM application, you are now able to present your mark in a wider range of electronic formats, such as in an MP3 or MP4 format. This defines protection for sound, moving images, hologram or a multimedia trade marks much more precisely than we previously possible. (Note– this change does not apply to UK designations filed through the International Madrid system).

2. Marks which consist exclusively of shapes cannot be registered if the shape itself performs a purely technical function, adds value to the goods or results from the nature of the goods. These provisions have now been extended to cover not just shapes, but any characteristic which is intrinsic to the goods applied for.

3. The UK IPO will no longer notify Applicants about similar expired third party trade mark registrations during the examination stage (Note – it is possible for expired UK

registrations to be restored or renewed, therefore, they could still pose a risk to the registration of your mark).

4. In relation to opposition proceedings, the five-year period where a mark used as basis for opposition can be challenged on the basis of non- use, now ends from the date your application was made or on its priority date as opposed to the date of publication of the application. This will apply to proceedings started on or after 14 January 2019, but not to those started before then.

As of 14 January 2019, a wider range of organisations will be able to apply for a collective trade mark in the UK. Furthermore, if you are an authorised user (of a collective mark), you will not be able to take legal action against infringement unless you have the permission of the proprietor of the collective trade mark, or there is an agreement in place allowing you to do so.

STEP 1: Before you apply
Search existing trade marks to see if there are any similar trade marks already in use which may affect your application for registration.
Check to see if it is a trade mark the IPO can accept.

STEP 2: Choose goods and services
Research and provide descriptions of the goods and/or services you are going to use your trade mark on. The Intellectual Property Office uses a classification system which divides the goods and services into 45 classes. See the IPO website for a detailed description of classifications.

*

STEP 3: Apply online – From £170 (2020-2021)

Choose from the following examination services:

- Standard examination (£170 when paid in full with one class of goods or service with £50 for each additional class)
- No refund if your trade mark cannot be registered
- Right start (£200 for one class of goods or services) - Pay 50% on application. £50 each additional class
- No refund, but only pay the balance if you decide to continue with the application.

The online application takes about 10 to 15 minutes to complete and you can 'Save for later' at any point.

For details of all other fees go to:
www.gov.uk/government/publications/trade-mark-forms-and-fees

After you apply

When the IPO receives your application, they check it to make sure it has all the information they need. If there are any problems with your form, they will contact you although they cannot refund your application fee or premium for any reason and you cannot alter your mark after you have sent in your application form. The IPO will capture your details onto their database. They then issue your filing receipt and application number within a few business days:

- by email for e-filed applications
- by post for paper filed applications

Examining your mark

When the application is complete and the appropriate fee has been paid, it will be sent to an examination team who will examine your mark.

Options following an objection

Depending on the objection raised, you have a variety of options in dealing with the objection. If you need more time to complete certain actions, you can apply for an Extension of Time.

What happens once my mark is accepted?

Once the IPO has accepted your trade mark they publish it in their weekly Trade Marks Journal and write to tell you the publication date and the number of that Journal.

Is your mark acceptable?

The examination of your application will decide whether it meets the requirements of the Trade Marks Act 1994 and Trade Mark Rules 2000 (as modified).

Earlier potentially conflicting trade marks

The IPO will search their register to identify earlier potentially conflicting trade marks. These are marks which may be the same or similar to your mark and for the same or similar goods or services

Your examination report

The IPO normally issues their examination report within around 30 days of receiving your application. In this report they list their objections and requirements and tell you how long you have to reply. You will have the opportunity to persuade the examiner that the objection(s) are not valid or to make amendments to your specification of goods and services. If the only problem with your mark is earlier rights, you only get one chance to discuss this with the IPO.

Publishing your mark

When your application has overcome any objections and you are happy to proceed, the IPO will publish your application in their Trade Mark Journal where your application is open to opposition for a 2 month period by any of the earlier marks they have notified, or any other party. This period can be extended to 3 months by anyone considering opposition.

Inspecting documents

The IPO will tell you how your trade mark application is progressing.   You can also check the status of your trade mark or trade mark application on their official register.

Check status

You can enter your trade mark number into the IPO number search to check the status of your trade mark or trade mark application.

Inspection of documents held in the Registry

You may inspect the register of trade mark documents filed at the registry after 31 October 1994 in relation to:

- an application filed on/after that date which has been published, or
- a registered mark.

However, some documents may be excluded from this provision under the terms of Rule 50, which provides a full list of excluded documents. The provisions in Rule 50 take precedence over the disclosure provisions of the Freedom of Information Act 2000, as they are one of the exemptions under section 44 of that Act.

To view documents

You should Contact the IPO and give notice of your visit to allow files to be retrieved from their stores. There is a handling charge of £5 per file which includes the cost of any prints taken, though the IPO can quote for their actual costs where particularly large files are involved.

To obtain copies of documents

If you are unable to visit the Office, you may request copies of the documents held on IPO files (subject to the inspection rights shown above), from Sales at the following address:

Intellectual Property Office
Concept House
Cardiff Road
Newport
South Wales
NP10 8QQ
Telephone 0300 300 2000

The cost is £5 per file copied, and £20 for certified copies, though again the IPO reserves the right to quote for their actual costs where particularly large files are involved

Managing Trade Marks

Renewing your trade mark and changing information

There are limited ways in which you can change the details of your trade mark and you must renew your trade mark every 10 years to keep it in force.

Please be aware that companies and individuals are sending misleading invoices to applicants and registered owners of trade marks. These communications may appear to be official but they are not linked to the Intellecual Property Office or any other Government organisation.

Renewing your trade mark

You can renew your trade mark for ever. However, to keep your trade mark in force, you must renew it on the 10th anniversary of the filing date and every 10 years after that.

Restoration

If you do not renew your trade mark in the 6 months after the renewal date, you have a further 6 months to apply to restore your registration.

Changing-

Transferring ownership (assigning)

You can transfer ownership of your trade mark to someone else. This includes any change of ownership as a result of company mergers.

Transfering ownership of Community trade marks

You can only transfer ownership of your Madrid or Community trade mark through OHIM or WIPO. This includes any change of ownership as a result of company mergers.

Appointment or change of representative

You can appoint or change a trade mark attorney at any time by completing the appropriate form.

Change of owner's name, addres or e mail address

If you change your name, address or email address, you should tell the IPO so that they can update the trade marks register.

Correcting an error

You may be able correct an obvious error in your application or trade mark registration.

Cancelling your trade mark

You can cancel your trade mark registration at any time.

Exploiting your trade marks
Licensing

A licence gives you permission to use someone else's trade marks. The terms of the licence are between you and the licensor and the IPO do not have any powers to investigate the validity of any licence you might agree. When your licence agreement ends or the licensees details are changed you should use the Form TM51 so that the IPO can record this on the register. There is a fee of £50 per form.

Mortgaging

You can use your trade mark as security for a loan. The mortgagor has a legal right in your trade mark until you repay the loan. You or your mortgagor should register the mortgage (security interest) with the IPO on form TM24 and they will then record it in the register. When it has been repaid they can cancel the details from the register. You can cancel the 'security interest' from the register by filing form TM24C.

You can also record a financial interest in someone else's registered trade mark. There is a fee of £50 per form although the fees are subject to change and should be checked..

Marketing

You may want to involve others to help exploit, develop or marketing your trade mark.

Certified and uncertified copies

The IPO will supply a copy of a trade mark or trade mark application, upon request and payment of the fee. You can also access the register on-line and get trade marks information at no cost.

Certified copies give proof that the IPO issued them.
Uncertified copies are photocopied documents.
What type of copy do I need?
You must use certified copies:

- when applying for a trade mark abroad
- when needed as evidence in a court of law, for example, if you are involved in legal action to enforce or defend your trade mark rights.

You can use **uncertified** copies for your personal reference or research.

Transferring or selling the ownership of a trade mark

If you transfer or sell the ownership of your trade mark or the ownership changes following company mergers, then you must tell the IPO by using the form TM16 so that they can record it on the register of trade marks. Assignment is the legal term for transferring ownership and the form TM16 is the form the IPO use to record this. It does not replace a formal assignment document. There is a £50 fee per form.

The form must be signed by you and the new proprietors. If this is not possible, then documentary evidence of the transfer of ownership must be provided. Send your request to the Intellectual Property Office, address as above.

What happens next?

The IPO will record the assignment in the register of trade marks and confirm this in writing

Enforcing your trade mark

Using the ® Symbol

You do not have to identify your trade mark as registered but you can use the ® symbol or the abbreviation "RTM" (for Registered Trade Mark) to show that your trade mark is registered, the mark can be registered somewhere other than in the United Kingdom.   The ® symbol is usually placed on the right-hand side of the trade mark, in a smaller type size than the mark itself, and in a raised (superscript) position; none of this is compulsory. If you do not have the ® symbol available, you can use the abbreviation "RTM".

You would break the law (Section 95 of the Trade Marks Act 1994) if you use the registered symbol ® or the abbreviation "RTM", on a mark that is not registered anywhere in the world.

Am I breaking the law by using "TM" on my trade mark?

No, as this does not indicate that your trade mark is actually registered, only that it is being used as a trade mark. The symbol 'TM' has no legal significance in the United Kingdom.

Resolving disputes

The IPO always encourages parties who are in dispute to resolve their differences before seeking a judgment by the office.

Before proceedings commence

Lord Woolf's 1996 report 'Access to Justice' identified the need for parties to see legal action as a last resort. He suggested that they should first try to settle matters outside the judicial system. These principles are reflected in the Civil Procedure Rules which were introduced in April 1999. In line with those Rules, if an action is launched before the Registrar and there is no prior contact between the parties, they may be penalised when the costs of the case are determined. So if you are thinking of taking legal action you should attempt to resolve the matter before launching any action.

Requests for stays or suspensions in inter partes proceedings

Where a stay or suspension is requested because the parties are trying to negotiate an amicable settlement, the parties will need to show what they have already done to resolve the dispute.

If the IPO is not satisfied that those negotiations are making progress they will not allow any further extensions to the stay of proceedings.

*

Hearing or written decision

When any period allowed for the filing of evidence is over the IPO will offer the parties either a hearing or a decision from the papers already filed. In either case the decision will resolve the dispute. The decision will be open to appeal.

Mediation

Mediation is another route that the IPO will be actively encouraging. It is another way that parties can resolve their dispute.

Cooling-off period

Gives both sides in potential opposition proceedings the chance to agree to settle their differences within a cooling-off period, without going through the full legal procedure.

The Company Names Tribunal

The Company Names Tribunal adjudicate on opportunistic company name registrations.

Counterfeiting of trade marks

If someone deliberately uses your registered trade mark, without your knowledge or consent, they may be guilty of the crime of counterfeiting.If there is sufficient evidence, the Police or Trading Standards Officers can take criminal proceedings under trade marks law. The IPO is not responsible for policing the Register of trade marks, and cannot advise you about what legal action to take to protect your mark.

If you suspect that someone is passing off, infringing, or counterfeiting goods or services under your mark, it is recommended that you consult your local Trading Standards

Office. You can also visit the official trading standards website for more information. You can also seek appropriate professional help, from a solicitor or a trade marks attorney.

European & International Trade mark's

If you want to use your trade mark in countries other than the United Kingdom, you can apply directly to the Trade Mark Office in each country. You can use a single application system to apply for an *International trade mark* (for certain countries throughout the world), or a *Community trade mark.* (for protection in Europe). Both these single application systems cover many countries including the United Kingdom and offer a number of other potential benefits, including:

- less to pay;
- less paperwork;
- lower agents' costs;
- faster results;
- easy application

The International route

You can apply to register your trade mark through the international route in countries which are party to the Madrid Protocol through the World Intellectual Property Organisation (WIPO). Currently more than 70 countries are members, including the United States of America, Australia and members of the European Union (EU).

Re-registration of UK marks in other countries

The IPO provides a list of web links that will direct you to their most up-to-date lists of the countries in which trade mark protection may be extended. You can access this list via the Professional Section of their website.

Using and buying trade marks

You may be able to buy or use other people's trade marks. If you want to use other people's trade marks, you usually need permission. If you use registered trade marks without permission, you are infringing the trade mark and the owner can take legal action against you and claim damages. If you want to use a registered trade mark, you can approach the owner to agree a licence with them. You may also be able to buy the trade marks rights from the owner. This results in transferring the ownership, or assigning it, to you.

Using

Infringing

If you use an identical or similar and confusable trade mark for identical or similar goods or services to a trade mark already in use - you are likely to be infringing the earlier mark. You can search IPO records to find the owner of a registered trade mark.

Registrable transactions

You can use certified copies to prove details about a trade mark or application. You can use uncertified copies for your personal reference or research.

Buying

Transferring ownership

If you buy a trade mark, you must tell the IPO that you are the new owner.

Ch. 7

Passing Off

The practice of 'passing off' involves one trader giving the impression that his goods are those of another trader who has an established goodwill. I am sure that we have all seen it, from fast food to sportswear to publications and so on. It also occurs where one trader indicates that his goods are of the same quality as another trader or where one trader creates the impression of association with another trader. Where an existing trader has a reputable or popular good or service, another trader will hope to take commercial advantage of the goodwill that has been built up. The first trader will suffer loss of sales and, subsequently, goodwill and loss if the goods are in any way substandard.

Honest traders are protected against these activities by the law of passing off. Passing off is a tort. It provides common law protection of brand names and get-up. This form of action is used either where the mark is an unregistered mark, or where the mark is unregistrable. For registered marks, the proprietor can bring an action for passing off as well as trade mark infringement. In court, the issues will be the same namely, there must be a balance between protecting the proprietor's goodwill, while protecting the interests of other legitimate traders. The interests of other consumers must also be considered.

The difference between infringing trademarks and passing off

Once a trademark has been registered, protection against infringement is automatic. Trademarks are a form of personal property and their use by another without permission constitutes interference with that person's property right. On the other hand, the claimant in a passing off action must demonstrate the presence of goodwill in order to have a right of action. The common law protects the goodwill of a business associated with a trade name or get-up, while trademark legislation protects rights in the actual name. The protection provided in passing off is potentially broader. Business goodwill can cover the name of the goods or services in question, business methods, get-up and marketing style.

Two cases sum up the difference in protection provided. In Coca-Cola Trademark Applications (1986) the House of Lords refused to allow the registration of the shape of the famous bottle, because it was concerned about the creation of a monopoly. In Reckitt and Coleman Products Ltd v Bordern Inc (1990) the same court restrained the defendants use of a plastic container resembling the defendants lemon in a passing off action. Registration of shapes, as discussed, is now allowed under the 1994 Trademarks Act.

The traditional form of passing off is where the defendant gives the consumer the impression that the goods sold are actually those of the claimant. A defendant may also be found to be passing off one quality of the claimant's goods as goods of another quality. In A.G. Spalding and Bros v A.W. Gammage Ltd (1915) the claimants manufactured 'Orb' footballs. They applied their mark to two types of ball, and sold the inferior type to waste rubber merchants. The defendant bought those inferior products and sold then in such a way as to imply that they were the higher quality 'orb' footballs. This was a clear case of passing off and was held to be so.

However, once a defendant has established goodwill in his own product using the claimant's name, it becomes very difficult to restrain him. In Vine Products Ltd v Mackenzie Ltd (1969) Spanish producers of sherry tried to stop the use of the name sherry on products from regions other than Jerez in Spain. However, in this case, producers in other countries and regions were able to show that they had already established goodwill in their sherry. As a result of this, the courts established that they were able to continue with the use of the name sherry, with the country of origin as a prefix.

The requirements of a passing off action

The minimum requirements for a successful action in passing off were laid down by Lord Diplock in Erven Warnink Besloven Vennootschap v J Townsend and Sons Ltd (1979). These were:

'(1) a misrepresentation (2) made by a trader in the course of trade (3) to prospective customers of his or ultimate customers of goods or services supplied by him, (4) which is calculated to injure the business or goodwill of another trader (in the sense that it is a reasonably foreseeable consequence) and (5) which causes actual damage to the business or goodwill of the trader by whom the action is brought will probably do so'

These five requirements were reduced to three by Reckitt and Coleman products v Bordern Ltd (1990) as: (a) the existence of claimants goodwill (b) a misrepresentation and (c) damage or likely damage to the claimants goodwill or reputation.

The claimant's goodwill

The claimant must establish goodwill associated with goods or their get-up. Goodwill has been defined as: 'the whole advantage, whatever it may be, of the reputation and connection of the firm which have been built up by the years of honest work or gained by lavish expenditure of money'. Trego v Hunt (1895). This interpretation has stood the test of time. Reputation is built up over time and customers develop loyalty and recognition of a product's inherent worth.

Goodwill can be localised. One business, say in Liverpool cannot really stop another business in Sussex using a name if it is local to a business, such as 'Cutters' hairdressing. However, if the business has a national or international reputation then this is a different matter.

A key case here is that of Scandecor Development AB v Scandecor Marketing AB (1998) which concerned whether a parent or subsidiary company owns the goodwill in a name.

The facts were that a Swedish poster company was split and set up a UK subsidiary trading under the name Scandecor which was the sole retailer in the UK. The UK company continued to obtain its poster from the Swedish company. the main principle arising out of the case was that the goodwill belongs to the company that either traded or exercised business control over activities in the UK.

Misrepresentation

The misrepresentation need not be intentional for a passing off action to succeed and innocence of misrepresentation is no defence. However, the defendant's state of mind may influence the remedy awarded by a court. The misrepresentation may be in respect of the origin of the goods, their quality or even the way in which they are made. Most of the cases of misrepresentation concern origin and quality. In Coombes International v Scholl (1977) the claimant manufactured insoles called 'Odor eaters' which contained activated charcoal. The defendant, who was a well-known manufacturer of footwear, also produced odour eaters. These were packaged in the same way. An injunction was granted on the basis that there was a misrepresentation as to the origins of the defendant's products, which was found to be inferior.

Another case was that of Arsenal Football Club plc v Reed (2001) which concerned the use of identical marks on identical goods. the facts of the case were that the defendant had, for over 30 years, sold memorabilia bearing the football club's name and logo. However, due to a disclaimer the defendant's customers realised that the goods neither came from nor were sanctioned by the club. They bought his products as badges of allegiance to the club. The disclaimer that was displayed was sufficient to prevent the misrepresentation necessary for a passing off. It was, however, insufficient to prevent consumers making a material link when the case was referred to the ECJ on the trade mark infringement issue. The main legal principle arising out of the case was that for passing off to have occurred customers or ultimate consumers must have been deceived with a real likelihood of confusion.

Misrepresentation and confusion
Confusion is by degree and the claimant in such a case would need evidence that the confusion is significant enough for an action to be brought.

Several well known cases highlight this. Neutrogena Corp and Another v Golden Ltd and Another (1996). The claimants sold a range of hypo-allergic products for the skin and hair under the name Neutrogena. The defendants started marketing a similar, but narrower range of skin and hair products under the name Neutralia. The claimants argued that use of the prefix 'Neutr' lead to confusion. Varied evidence of confusion was demonstrated. This included complaints about a Neutralia advertisement, which the complainants had taken to be for Neutrogena. Other evidence was produced, of a substantial nature and the courts held that the legal test on the issue of deception was whether, on a balance of probabilities, a substantial number of members of the public would be misled into purchasing the defendants product in the belief that it was the claimant's. The court felt that the evidence produced demonstrated confusion caused by the defendants' mark.

Two other recent cases are of interest here. Firstly, Robyn Rihanna Fenty (Rihanna) and others v Arcadia Group Brands Limited (Topshop) 2013. In this case, whilst the Judge found in favour of the claimant, Miss Robyn Rihanna Fenty (Rihanna) the pop singer, in her claim for passing off, the legal principle in the UK, made clear by the judge, remains that there is "*no such thing as a freestanding general right by a famous person, or anyone else, to control the reproduction of their image*".

The Judge made it clear that it was the peculiarities of "*this image of this person on this garment by this shop in these circumstances*" that led him to conclude that a substantial number of consumers will be confused into thinking that Rihanna had authorised that T-shirt.

This case, as all cases was taken on its own merit but the judge was unambiguous in stating that " *the mere sale of a t-shirt by a trader bearing an image of a famous person is not, without more, an act of passing off*".

In a second case highlighting this, Hearst v AVELA et al (2014), the same Judge, although finding against the defendants, again reiterated the principle stated above that there is no freestanding right by a famous or other person to control the

103

reproduction of their image. This case involved the claimants Hearst Holdings Inc and Fleischer Studios Inc ("Hearst"). Hearst were the successors of the originators of the cartoon character Betty Boop. They licensed Betty Boop merchandise in the UK. The defendants AVELA were accused of passing off and the Judge found in Hearts favour although reiterating the same principle in relation to images as the Rihanna case.

Confusion and common fields of activity

Traditionally, there was a need for the claimant and defendant to be in the same field of business activity before it was considered likely that there would be confusion leading to injury and goodwill. This qualification has prevented some individuals from stopping the unauthorised use of their name. In McCulloch v May (1947) the claimant was a well-known children's broadcaster who used the name 'Uncle Mac'. The defendant sold cereal under the name 'Uncle Mac' alluding to some of the claimant's characteristics, without his permission. The claimant failed in his action for passing off as he was not involved in the making or marketing of cereals. According to the court, there had to be a common field of activity in which, however remotely, the claimant and defendant were engaged.

The need for a common field of activity to be established before action can be taken has had a detrimental effect on the commercial practice of character merchandising. This is where the names or pictures of famous characters, whether real or fictional, are applied to everyday goods to make them more marketable.

In Lynstad v Anabus Products Ltd (1977) the members of the group ABBA were unable to stop their pictures being applied to T shirts because they were in the entertainment business and not in the same field of manufacturers of clothing. However, there is a general move away from this rigid approach to character merchandising which will be discussed further on.

Inverse passing off

Inverse passing off occurs where the defendant falsely claims that the claimant's goods or services are actually made or provided by the defendant. A Key case here is Bristol Conservatories Ltd v Conservatories Custom Built Ltd (1989). The facts were that the defendant's sales representatives showed potential customers photographs of conservatories as a sample of the defendant's workmanship. the photographs were, in fact, of the claimant's conservatories. The main finding in this case was that the misdescription harmed the claimant's goodwill and constituted passing off.

Post-sale confusion

Post-sale confusion is where the misrepresentation comes after the goods have been purchased. Even if there is no deception at the time of sale, later confusion as to the origin of the name, mark or device can still damage the goodwill by a process of dilution or erosion.

Damage

The claimant must show damage or a probability of damage. The damage need not be tangible. A claimant can employ a range of methods to prove confusion leading to lost sales or dilution of reputation. One method is the use of surveys although this is not seen as a reliable way of providing evidence. If surveys are used they should be properly carried out otherwise the results may be discredited by the courts. Therefore, good statistical methods should be employed.

Domain names

Domain names are the internet addresses registered by users of the internet. They perform similar functions to trademarks. However, the domain name system is far less flexible than that for registration of trademarks. Each name given is unique so that there is little scope for other businesses to use it. The courts, when dealing with domain names have shown a willingness to allow actions for passing off and trademark infringement under s.10 (3).

One case, British Telecommunications Plc v One in a Million Ltd and Other's (1999) the defendant had registered a large number of domain names comprising the names or trade marks of well known businesses without asking permission. None were in use as active websites. The defendants had registered them with a view to selling them to the owners of the goodwill or collectors.

Among the brands concerned were Marks and Spencers, Sainsbury, Ladbrokes, Virgin and British Telecom. These companies sued the defendants alleging passing off and trademark infringement.

In Marks and Spencer's case the Court of Appeal were of the opinion that the use of the name in a domain created the impression that the defendants were somehow involved or linked to Marks and Spencer. Although the other cases were slightly different the Court of Appeal held in favour of the claimants and infringement was upheld.

Injurious falsehood

In between the torts of defamation and passing off there is injurious falsehood. The action is also referred to as malicious. It is linked to passing off because it is another form of protection for a trader's goodwill. It is also defamation because the defendant has, allegedly, libelled the business of another trader. To succeed, the claimant must show that the defendant maliciously made false statements about the claimant's goods or services, which were calculated to cause damage. If the defendant's statements about the claimant's goods is true, there is no action, the onus is on the claimant to prove that the statement is false.

Remedies

Damages are available in a passing off action. These are usually based on the actual loss suffered as far as that can be calculated. Damages may also be calculated on a royalty basis, in other words the amount that the defendant would have paid if he had applied for a licence to use the claimant's name or mark. It is also the norm to obtain an injunction to restrain defendants activities.

****

Ch. 8

Character Merchandising

Character merchandising is a very significant business activity amounting to many millions of pounds. It is, essentially, the practice of using the name and/or image of a popular character, whether real or fictional, to promote products.

The way character merchandising should work is that an organisation specialising in merchandising will obtain a licence from the creator of the character which allows for the representation of that character on a certain product, in return for a licence fee. Some traders will avoid paying a fee and will use the character anyway and can sell their goods at a lower price than a licensed trader. In addition, quality becomes an issue, as unlicensed traders will not have to conform to any standard.

The legal protection against unauthorised use of characters is not very clear. In passing off, protection has been hampered by the need to establish a common field of activity between the owner of the character and the person using it.

Character merchandising and defamation

In certain cases, an actual person can stop unauthorised use of their character by suing for defamation. An example of an action of this sort is Tolley v Fry (1931). The claimant was an amateur golfer. His picture was used by the defendants to advertise their chocolate without consent. They were subsequently sued for libel. The claimant successfully claimed that anyone using his picture would think that he had compromised his amateur status by accepting money for advertising. Tolley succeeded because it was held that 'the defendants had published a false statement which lowered him in the estimation of right thinking members of society'. The advertisement suggested that he had compromised his amateur status and so fell within the standard definition of defamation.

Defamation, however, is only a viable course of action if a name has been used to promote something undesirable.

Character merchandising and copyright

Copyright offers some protection. Section 1 (1)(a) of the Copyrights, Designs and Patents Act 1988, states that copyright subsists in 'original literary, dramatic, musical or artistic works'. The owners of a character can protect its image, under the Act as an artistic work. Under s.4, photographs and drawings are included as artistic works. Anybody making a copy of the work, or issuing copies of it to the public without the copyright owner's permission, is guilty of infringement according to ss..17-18. So putting an unauthorised copy of a cartoon on a T-shirt would amount to an infringement, as would selling the T-shirt bearing a copy of that cartoon.

Copyright does have its limitations. There are difficulties where only the name of a character is used, as there is no copyright or titles, no matter how distinctive. Even if a picture of a character is used, the copyright owner must show that the representation is an exact or substantial copy, as copyright protects the expression of an idea and not the idea itself. Where the representation is a photograph of a real personality, the personality will only be able to use copyright to protect his image if the copyright in the photograph has been assigned to

109

him, as, since 1st August 1988, the copyright in a photograph usually belongs to the person taking it.

A case highlighting an attempt to use copyright to protect a personality's features, is the case of Merchandising Corp of America v Harpbond (1983). This case concerned the group Adam and the Ants and in particular the distinctive face make up worn by the lead singer. The claimant sued the defendants for reproducing the pictures of Adam Ant with his distinctive make up claiming that the make up was a copyright work (a painting). This argument was rejected by the court

Character merchandising and registered trademarks

Since the passing of the 1994 Trademarks Act, personalities can apply to register their names, caricatures and any other identifying mark. Examples of trademarks that have been applied for or registered are Paul Gascoigne's application to register a caricature of himself and also the name 'Shearer' and the number 9 shirt.

Character merchandising and passing off

The use of passing off as a form of protection has been hindered by the notion of 'common field of activity'. In Wombles Ltd v Wombles Skips (1977) the case concerned the Wombles who were fictitious characters well known for clearing up litter. The defendants formed a company to hire out skips, and used the name 'Wombles' because of the connection to tidiness. The claimant claimed a common field of activity in their claim as the Wombles had granted a licence to reproduce the Wombles on wastepaper baskets. The case failed because the courts held that there was no common field of activity.

Another important case was that of Taverner Rutledge v Trexapalm Ltd (1977) concerning the TV character Kojak, famous for sucking lollipops. The claimant made lollipops similar in shape to those used by Kojak and sold them as 'Kojakpops'. It quickly established goodwill in the name for the products, yet did not have, and had not sought a licence from the TV company responsible for the series. The defendants, who obtained a licence from the company created lollipops, called Kojak lollies. The claimants sued for passing off. Although it was argued that the defendants licence, with quality control terms illustrated a connection in the course of business and the owners of the name, in other words a common field of activity, this argument failed because there was no actual or potential common field of activity between the owners of the television series and the defendants business, there being no evidence of the exercise of quality control by the owners of the series.

According to the Judge, the defendant would have to show that the practice of character merchandising had become so well know that as soon as anybody in the street realised that a product was licensed by the owners of some series, like Kojak, he would say to himself not only 'this must have been licensed by them' but also ' and that is a guarantee of its quality'. In this case, the claimant's lollies were of better value and quality than the defendant's product, which would have harmed the claimant's reputation.

The reference to quality control is important in that it indicates a way to get around the problems of common field of activity. Stricter quality control exercised through the terms of a licence should indicate an active interest in the type of goods being produced and thereby form the necessary connection in the course of trade.

The case involving Mirage Studios v Counter Feat Clothing Co Ltd (1991) illustrates recognition that the public are well aware of the practice of character merchandising. The claimants created the 'Teenage Mutant Ninja Turtle' characters. They also made and marketed cartoons, films and videos containing these characters. Part of the claimants business involved licensing the reproduction of the images. Without the claimant's permission the defendant made drawings, similar to the Ninja Turtles but not exact reproductions and licensed the use of these. The courts granted an injunction against the defendants stating that a misrepresentation had taken place because there was evidence to show that a substantial number of the buying public expected, and knew, where a famous cartoon or television character was reproduced on goods, that reproduction was the result of a licence granted by the owner of the copyright or owner of other rights in the character. It was held:

'Since the public associated the goods with the creator of the characters, the depreciation of the image by fixing the Turtles picture to inferior goods and inferior material might seriously reduce the value of the licensing rights'. This decision has been generally welcomed and should help somewhat to clear up problems associated with the notion of 'common field of activity'.

****

Ch. 9

Copyright

Copyright and Britain's withdrawal from the EU

At the end of this chapter, there is a summary of the changes to copyright law as a result of the UK's exit from the EU. the changes come into affect from 1st of January 2021 and are significant and will affect many areas of copyright law.

Definition of copyright

Copyright is the right to prevent others copying or reproducing an individuals or other's work. *Copyright protects the expression of an idea and not the idea itself.* Only when an idea is committed to paper can it be protected. Others can be directly or indirectly stopped from copying the whole or a substantial part of a copyright work. However, others cannot be stopped from borrowing an idea or producing something very similar.

Copyright is a right that arises automatically upon the creation of a work that qualifies for copyright protection. This means that there is no registration certificate to prove ownership. To claim ownership the author will have to produce original and preferably dated evidence of the creation of the work and proof of authorship. The author will also need to show that he/she is a qualifying person and that the work was produced in a convention country.

To be a qualifying person (s.154 of the Copyright Designs and Patents Act 1988) the author must have been, at the material time, a British Citizen, subject or protected person, a British

Dependant territories citizen, a British national (overseas) or a British Overseas Citizen or must have been resident or domiciled in a convention country at the material time, which is when the work was first published. If the author dies before publication the material time is before his death. A convention country is a country that is signatory to the Universal Copyright Convention or the Berne Copyright Convention, which includes most countries in the world.

The works that can qualify for protection are defined in S.1 of the 1988 Act. These are:

a) Original literary, dramatic, musical and artistic works
b) Sound recordings, films, broadcasts and cable programmes
c) Typographical arrangements of published editions

Historical background

Copyright has its origins in the 16th century. The courts recognised a need for some form of protection for books. In 1556, a system of registration of books was established to offer protection for authors. If an author registered a book with the Stationers Company it gave him/her a perpetual right to reproduce the book and prevent reproduction by anyone else. For almost 200 years this form of protection only applied to books. In 1734 this extended to engravings (Engravings Copyright Act) A number of Acts were passed over the next 150 years extending copyright protection to musical, dramatic and artistic works. In 1875, a Royal Commission was set up to look at the position and recommended a clear approach be adopted to copyright protection, codified into one single Act. This happened after Great Britain signed the Berne Copyright Convention in 1885.

The Berne Convention provided for international protection of copyright for the work of all nationals of all countries signing the convention. It also required each member country to extend minimum standards of protection to nationals of all other member countries.

The United Kingdom implemented the 1911 Copyright Act to put into place minimum standards and also draw together previous legislation. The next Act, prompted by changes in the Berne Convention led to the 1956 Copyright Act. This Act reflected changes, amongst other things, in the field of technology. In 1973, the Whitford Committee was appointed to review the state of copyright law. The Committee reported in 1977 suggesting numerous changes to the law, resulting in a Green paper in 1981, 'Reform of the law relating to Copyright, Designs and Performers Protection' and subsequently the White Paper 'Intellectual Property and Innovation' which led to the 1988 Copyright Designs and Patents Act, which was a consolidating Act and which has been amended.

Since the Act came into force in August 1989, there have been a number of amending regulations dealing with implementation of EC Directives on rights to reproduce copyright software as is necessary for lawful use, protection of semiconductor chip topography rights and harmonisation of copyright duration. There are further legislative moves afoot to update copyright law to deal with the growth of new technology.

See the end of this chapter for an overview of significant amendments which have been made to the Act by new regulations introduced in 2014. The below deals with the main body of the 1988 Act.

Copyright – subsistence of copyright

As shown above, copyright is a property right that subsists in certain works. It is a statutory right giving the copyright owner certain exclusive rights in relation to his or her work.

In the 1988 Copyright Designs and Patents Act, as amended, there are nine categories of copyright works:

'Authorial' 'Primary' or 'LDMA' works

1) Literary works
2) Dramatic works
3) Musical works
4) Artistic works

'Entrepreneurial' 'Secondary' or 'Derivative' works

5) Sound recordings
6) Films
7) Broadcasts
8) Cable programmes
9) Typographical arrangements of published editions (the typography right)

Copyright comes into existence, or subsists automatically where a qualifying person creates a work that is original and tangible (or fixed).

Qualification

Copyright will not subsist in a work unless:

a) It has been created by a qualifying person
b) It was first published in a qualifying country
c) In the case of literary, dramatic and musical works, the work must be fixed, that is reduced to a material form in writing or otherwise.

Copyright works

The CDPA 1988 defines a literary work as being 'any work written, spoken or sung, other than a dramatic or musical work'. A novel or poem could equally fall into this category. Additionally, the concept of literary works extends to tables (e.g. a rail timetable) compilations such as directories and computer programmes. Databases are also regarded as literary works. In essence, any work that can be expressed in print, irrespective of quality, will be a literary work.

Dramatic works

The CDPA 1988 defines 'dramatic works' as including works of dance or mime. In the case Norowzian v Arks (1999) it was stated that these terms should be given their natural and ordinary meaning, the implication being that dramatic works are works of *action*. The courts also recognised in this case that films may be produced as dramatic works, either as dramatic works in themselves and/or as a recording of a dramatic work.

Musical works

A musical work is a work consisting solely of musical notes, any words or actions intended to be sung, spoken or recorded with the notes are excluded. Therefore, a melody is a musical works with the lyrics being literary.

Artistic works

A wide-ranging definition of artistic works is provided by the CDPA 1988 s.4. Works of architecture are included but focus is usually placed on the remaining artistic works. These fall into two categories:

a) Works protected irrespective of their artistic merit:

i) Graphic works, i.e. paintings, drawings, diagrams, maps, charts, plans, engravings, etchings, lithographs, woodcuts or similar works

ii) Photographs

iii) Sculptures. The protection of functional objects, such as a cast is problematic. In one notable case in New Zealand Wham-O manufacturing Co v Lincoln Industries Ltd (1985) a wooden model of a Frisbee was held to be a sculpture. The modern UK position is almost certainly more restrictive, as objects will not now be protected as sculptures where they are not made for the purpose of sculpture.

iv) Collages. Collages are artistic or functional visual arrangements produced by affixing two or more items together. Intrinsically ephemeral arrangements (for example the composition of a photograph) are not collages.

b) Artistic works required to be of a certain quality (CDPA 1988 s.4 (1) c i.e. works of artistic craftsmanship. Few works can meet the standard of artistic craftsmanship, as they must be both of artistic quality and the result of craftsmanship. These principles were further developed into a two-part test for artistic craftsmanship in Merlet v Mothercare (1986). First, did the creation of the work involve craftsmanship in the sense that skill and pride was invested in its manufacturer?

Second, does the work have aesthetic appeal and did an artist create it?

Sound recordings

A sound recording is a reproducible recording of either:

1) Sounds where there is no underlying copyright work (e.g. birdsong)
2) A recording of the whole or any part of a literary, dramatic or musical work.

The format of recording is of no relevance.

Film

The CDPA 1988 s.5B (1) provides that a film is a reproducible recording of a moving image on any medium. It is the recording itself that is protected, rather than the subject matter that has been recorded, but it should be borne in mind that a film might also be protected as a dramatic work. Film soundtracks are taken to be part of the film itself.

Broadcasts

Copyright subsists in sounds and visual images that are broadcast CDPA 1988 s.6 (1), a broadcast being defined as a transmission by wireless telegraphy of visual images, sounds or other information. The definition of 'broadcast' therefore encompasses radio and television broadcasts and both terrestrial and satellite broadcasting.

Cable programmes

The transmission of an item that forms part of a cable programme will create separate works that are capable of protection as cable programmes CDPA 1988 s.7. A cable programme service is defined as a service consisting wholly or mainly in sending visual images, sounds or other information via a telecommunications system which may utilise wires or microwave transmission. Items sent via wireless telegraphy are specifically excluded as they are already protected as broadcasts. This means that as well as subscription channels a website on the internet may be a cable programme service.

The typography right

The CDPA 1988 s.8 affords protection to the typography, that is the layout, of published editions of literary, dramatic and musical works. The leading authority on typographical arrangement copyright is Newspaper Licensing Agency Ltd v Marks and Spencer Plc (2001).

Copyright works the ideas/expression dichotomy

There is no copyright in ideas. Copyright subsists in the tangible expression of ideas and not the ideas themselves. In America this is referred to as the ideas/expression dichotomy. This principle can be helpful but should not be taken too literally, as whilst it is clear that mere ideas cannot be protected by copyright the following points should be noted:

1) What might be termed 'highly developed ideas', for example an early draft of a textbook, would be protected by copyright, as are preparatory design material for computer programmes.
2) Copyright cannot be circumvented by selectively altering the expression of a copyright work in the process of reproducing it.

Originality

The CDPA 1988 s.1 requires that literary, dramatic, musical and artistic works be 'original'. The originality requirements only apply to LDMA works, there is no such requirement for secondary copyright works, although it is clear that no copyright will subsist in secondary copyright works that merely reproduce secondary works.

LDMA works must be original in the sense that they originate with the author. One such case that highlights this is University of London Press v University Tutorial Press (1916). This is a minimal qualitative requirement: original works need not be inventive or original and a wide range of works have been held to be original, from coupons for football pools (Ladbrokes v William Hill (1964) to a compilation of broadcasting programmes (Independent Television Publications Ltd and the BBC v Time Out Ltd (1984).

Expending skill and judgement in creating an LDMA work usually suffices to deem the work original. Mere copying cannot confer originality. Alternatively, the mere expenditure of effort or labour (the so-called 'sweat of the brow' test for originality) has sometimes been said to be sufficient to confer originality. But in practice some minimum element of originality is required. For example, in Crump v Smythson (1944) it was held that the generic nature of commonplace diary material left no room for judgement in selection and arrangement therefore the resultant works were not original. Originality has also been held to be more than 'competent draftsmanship' (Interlego v Tyon 1988). Commonly databases and computer programmes were the subject matter of sweat of the brow concerns.

Higher standards of originality: computer programs and databases

As a result of two European Directives, The Directive on the Legal Protection of Databases (Directive 96/9/EC) and the Computer Directive (Directive 91/250/EEC) both computer programmes and databases must be original in the sense that they are the author's own intellectual creation. This is a higher standard or originality than that of 'skills, labour and judgement'.

Some databases may not meet the standard of originality to be afforded copyright protection. In this case the database can be protected by virtue of the *sui generis* database right. (See end of chapter and the UK's exit from the EU.)

The Database Directive which was incorporated into UK law by Part 11 of the Copyright and Rights in databases regulations 1997 grant a property right in a database whether or not it qualifies for a copyright work. The definition of database includes:

'a collection of independent works, data or other materials arranged in a systematic or methodical way and individually accessible by electronic or other means'.

A database can also be recognised as a literary work and thus afforded copyright protection. For this the database must be original and the contents and arrangements of the database must be a result of the author's own intellectual creation. In any case, all databases are protected by the new database rights irrespective of whether they qualify for copyright protection or not. To qualify for database rights the data must have been assembled through substantial investment in obtaining, verifying and presenting the contents. One case that illustrates this is British Horseracing Board Ltd v William Hill Organisation (2001)).

The duration of the database rights is for 15 years from 1st January of the year following completion of its making, or the first making public of the database within the 15 year period from its making.

Originality and the *de minimis principle*

The question arises, does copyright exist in very short works. The case, Exxon Corporation v Exxon Ind (1982), where the invented word Exxon was denied copyright protection, is often cited to support the proposition that a de minimis principle applies in copyright law, i.e. that some things are too small to be deemed copyright works. However, the authority for this is not so clear.

Fixation and tangibility

As we have seen, copyright does not subsist in literary, dramatic or musical works until they are recorded in writing or otherwise. This pragmatic requirement is known as 'fixation'. Usually, such works will be fixed by the author, but fixation by a third party (with or without the authors permission is also possible. Other copyright works are not subject to the fixation requirement. This is usually unproblematic as films, sound recordings, broadcasts, cable programmes and typography are inherently tangible works.

Ownership of copyright and the employee

The rule is that the first owner of copyright in a work is the person who created the work, i.e. the author. A major exception to this rule is CDPA 1988 s.11 (2). Which provides that where a person creates an LDMA work in the course of employment the employer is the first owner of any copyright in the work subject to any agreement to the contrary. There are special provisions for Crown use, Parliamentary copyright and copyright for certain international organisations (CDPA 1988 s.11 (3).

Authorship, ownership and moral rights

The author is the person who creates the work. Identifying the author is usually a straightforward task. The following is the standard authorship position:

- Literary work. The writer
- Dramatic work. The writer
- Musical work. The composer
- Artistic work. The artist
- Computer generated LDMA works. The person operating the computer.
- Sound recordings. The producer.
- Films. The producer and principal director.
- Broadcasts. The broadcaster.
- Cable programmes. The cable program service provider.
- Typography right. The publisher.
- Any work where the identity of the author is unknown. A work of unknown authorship.

Joint authorship

Where more than one person is involved in the creation of a work, careful consideration is needed in determining individual contributions. A person who suggests a subject to a poet is not the author of the poem. Merely supplying ideas is insufficient for joint authorship; an integral role in the expression of ideas is required. Joint authorship arises where the efforts of the two authors is indistinguishable.

BREXIT and changes to copyright law from 1st of January 2021

Copyright is a national right that each country provides separately. However, copyright is largely harmonised internationally by a number of treaties and, in the EU, by a body of EU copyright legislation that builds on the international treaties.

A substantial part of UK copyright law was derived from the EU's legislation when the UK was a member state. Because of this, there are references in UK law to the EU, the EEA, and member states. Some of these are in the UK's implementation of EU cross-border copyright arrangements. These arrangements apply only within the EU and EEA and provide reciprocal protections and benefits between member states.

To address this issue, the Government introduced the Intellectual Property (Copyright and Related Rights) (Amendment) (EU Exit) Regulations 2019 (Intellectual Property (Copyright and Related Rights) (Amendment) (EU Exit) Regulations 2019) under the powers of the European Union (Withdrawal) Act 2018, which came into force on 1 January 2021.

These regulations remove or correct references to the EU, EEA, or member states in UK copyright legislation and preserve the effect of UK law where possible.

The reciprocal cross-border arrangements will be amended or brought to an end, as appropriate and this outline explains their status from 1 January 2021.

Protection of UK copyright works in the EU

The majority of UK and EU copyright works (such as books, films and music) will still be protected in each other's territories because of their participation in the international treaties on copyright. This applies to works made before and after 1 January 2021.

Copyright clearance in satellite broadcasting

The EU Satellite and Cable Directive provides a country-of-origin principle for licensing of copyright material in cross-border satellite broadcasts. This means that when a satellite broadcaster transmits a copyright work, e.g. a film, from one EEA (European Economic Area) state to another, they are only required to get the copyright holder's permission for the state in which the broadcast originates. This avoids satellite broadcasters having to secure individual licences for every member state in which their broadcasts are received.

Actions for UK satellite broadcasters

UK broadcasters may no longer benefit from the country-of-origin principle for broadcasts into the EEA from 1 January 2021 and might need to get additional right holder permissions covering the EEA states to which they broadcast.

This will depend on how the domestic legislation of each EEA member state treats broadcasts originating in non-EEA countries - for example, whether they apply the country-of-origin principle to non-EEA broadcasts, as UK law does.

UK broadcasters should:

- check the domestic legislation of each EEA member state into which they broadcast to identify how they treat broadcasts originating in non-EEA countries

- consider whether their licensing arrangements will need to change after 1 January 2021 to allow them to continue to broadcast into the EEA

Broadcast of works transmitted into the UK

In the UK, the country-of-origin principle will continue to be applied to broadcasts from any country. Legitimate satellite broadcasts of copyright works transmitted into the UK from abroad will not need specific right holder permission for the UK, except where both of the following apply:

- the broadcast is commissioned or uplinked to a satellite in the UK
- it originates from a country that provides lower levels of copyright protection

Sui generis database rights

As we have seen, there are two types of intellectual property protection for databases: sui generis database rights (or just 'database rights') and copyright. Both are automatic, unregistered rights that allow the owner to control certain uses of their database.

Copyright protects the selection or arrangement of material in a database where this is original (i.e. creative). Database rights protect the contents of a database. A database does not have to be original for it to qualify for database rights, but there needs to have been a substantial investment in obtaining, verifying or presenting the data.

Database rights were introduced by the Database Directive. Eligible databases receive protection in all European Economic Area (EEA) member states. Only databases made by EEA nationals, residents or businesses are eligible.

The UK implemented the directive through the Copyright and Rights in Databases Regulations 1997.

Database rights from 1 January 2021

UK citizens, residents, and businesses will not be eligible to receive or hold database rights in the EEA for databases created on or after 1 January 2021. UK owners of databases created on or after 1 January 2021 will need to consider whether they can rely on alternative means of protection in the EEA – for example licensing agreements or copyright, where applicable.

UK legislation will be amended so that only UK citizens, residents, and businesses are eligible for database rights in the UK for databases created on or after 1 January 2021.

Existing database rights

Database rights that exist in the UK or EEA before 1 January 2021 (whether held by UK or EEA persons or businesses) will continue to exist in the UK and EEA for the rest of their duration. These rights are guaranteed under the Withdrawal Agreement.

Those in the UK who wish to use databases protected by these rights will continue to need the permission of the right holder(s).

Copyright in databases

Copyright protection for databases in the UK and EEA will not change after 1 January 2021. The UK and all EEA member states are members of international treaties on copyright that ensure eligible works (e.g. databases that are original) are protected in all treaty countries. This does not depend on the UK's relationship with the EU or EEA.

Copyright

Portability of online content services

The EU Portability Regulation allows consumers across the European Economic Area (EEA) to access their online content services (for example, video-on-demand streaming services, such as Netflix and Amazon Prime) as if they are at home when they travel within the EEA.

This means that an online service provider must provide customers the same content as in their home state when they are temporarily present in another state. The regulation applies only to travel between EEA member states.

Cross-border portability from 1 January 2021

The EU Portability Regulation will cease to apply to UK-EEA travel from 1 January 2021. In the UK, the regulation will be revoked. Online content service providers will not be required under the regulation to provide content ordinarily available in the UK to a UK customer who is temporarily present in any other EEA Member State.

This will not prevent service providers offering cross-border portability to their customers on a voluntary basis, but to do so they will need the permission of the owners of the content they provide.

Changes for UK customers of online content services

UK customers visiting the EEA and EEA customers visiting the UK may see restrictions to the content available to them from 1 January 2021. This will depend on the terms of their services and the licences in place between service providers and right holders.

Orphan works copyright exception

Orphan works are copyright works for which the right holder is not known or cannot be found. Because orphan works are protected by copyright, they cannot be used freely, even though it may be impossible to get the right holder's permission.

Under the EU Orphan Works Directive, cultural heritage institutions – e.g. libraries, archives and museums – based in the European Economic Area (EEA) can digitise and make orphan works available online across all EEA member states without the permission of the right holder.

Cultural heritage institutions must register orphan works used under the exception on a database maintained by the European Union Intellectual Property Office (EUIPO).

Orphan works exception from 1 January 2021

The EU orphan works exception will no longer apply to UK-based institutions and will be repealed from UK law from 1 January 2021. UK institutions may face claims of copyright infringement if they make orphan works available online in the UK or EEA, including works they had placed online before 1 January 2021.

Actions for UK cultural heritage institutions

By 1 January 2021 UK cultural heritage institutions will need to:

- remove any orphan works currently placed online under the exception
- consider seeking a licence under the UK's orphan works licensing scheme
- where they have a licence to use the work in the UK, consider limiting online access to users based in the UK to avoid copyright infringement in the EEA

Changes for UK orphan works scheme licensees

The UK's orphan works licensing scheme allows orphan works to be licensed in the UK for commercial and non-commercial uses, subject to the user paying application and licence fees and completing a diligent search for the right holder. Licensees will no longer need to consult the EUIPO orphan works database as part of the diligent search. No other changes will be made to the diligent search requirements or the licensing scheme in general.

Access to copyright works for visually impaired people from 1 January 2021

Cross-border exchanges of accessible format works for visually impaired or otherwise print-disabled people may change.

The Marrakesh Treaty to facilitate access to published works for persons who are blind, visually impaired or otherwise print disabled, is an international agreement to improve the access of visually impaired people to copyright works around the world.

The EU is party to the treaty and has implemented it via a directive and a regulation:

- the directive allows people in the EU with visual impairments and authorised bodies that support them (for example charities) to make or distribute accessible format copies of copyright works. The Regulation allows the import and export of such copies between EU member states and other treaty countries. The UK implemented the directive via the Copyright and Related Rights (Marrakesh Treaty etc.) Regulations 2018.

The Marrakesh Treaty from 1 January 2021

The regulation and the UK's implementation of the directive will be retained in UK law from 1 January 2021. In the UK, people with visual impairment or authorised bodies will still be able to make and distribute accessible format copies of copyright works. However, the cross-border exchange of accessible format copies of works may be affected. The UK has now ratified the Marrakesh Treaty in its own right, the UK's ratification of the treaty came into force on 1 January 2021.

Collective rights management from 1 January 2021

EEA collective management organisations may not automatically represent UK right holders and collective management organisations from 1 January 2021. Collective management organisations (CMOs) are not-for-profit and/or member-governed bodies that license rights on behalf of copyright owners.

CMOs in the European Economic Area (EEA) are governed by the Collective Rights Management (CRM) Directive. This includes obligations to represent on request right holders from any EEA member state unless there are objectively justified reasons not to do so. The Directive also requires EEA CMOs that offer multi-territorial licensing of musical works for online services to represent on request the catalogues of other EEA CMOs that do not offer those licences.

The UK implemented the CRM Directive via the Collective Management of Copyright (EU Directive) Regulations 2016. The government published guidance on those regulations.

Collective rights management from 1 January 2021

From 1 January 2021, EEA CMOs will not be required by the CRM Directive to represent UK right holders or to represent the catalogues of UK CMOs for online licensing of musical rights.

UK right holders and CMOs will still be able to request representation, but EEA CMOs may be free to refuse those requests depending on the law in individual member states.

In the UK, existing obligations on UK CMOs will be maintained following 1 January 2021. These include those specific to multi-territorial licensing of musical works for online services.

UK CMOs that offer multi-territorial licensing of online rights in musical works will continue to be required to represent on request the catalogue of other CMOs (UK or EEA) for multi-territorial licensing purposes.

Artist's resale right

The Artist's resale right entitles creators of artistic works to a royalty payment each time their works are sold by an art market professional. The UK implemented the EU's Resale Right Directive through the Artist's Resale Right Regulations 2006. These regulations were amended to reflect the UK's position outside the EU, while continuing to provide the right to foreign nationals on a reciprocal basis.

Nationals of the UK and other countries that provide reciprocal treatment for UK nationals (including EU member states) will continue to receive resale rights in the UK and those countries from 1 January 2021. This is in accordance with the Berne Convention. No changes are being made to the calculation of royalty payments.

Cable retransmissions of works

When a copyright work is broadcast between EEA member states and retransmitted by cable in the receiving member state, the copyright holder(s) can only exercise their rights through a collective management organisation. The UK applies this rule to cable retransmissions of broadcasts from EEA member states.

From 1 January 2021, member states may no longer apply this rule to broadcasts originating in the UK because it will no longer be a member state. Copyright holders whose works are broadcast from the UK and retransmitted via cable in the EEA:

- may need to negotiate licences with the cable operator directly
- could see statutory licensing terms imposed on the cable retransmission of their works in certain EEA states

UK legislation will continue to apply existing rules to cable retransmissions of broadcasts originating in an EEA member state.

Qualification for copyright protection

Works that are currently eligible for copyright protection in the UK will continue to be eligible from 1 January 2021. Works are eligible for copyright protection in the UK if they are:

- made by a national of the UK, EEA or any country that is party to the international copyright treaties

or

- first published or transmitted in the UK, EEA or any country that is party to the international copyright treaties

References to the EEA have been removed from UK law. This will not stop EEA works qualifying for copyright protection in the UK, because all EEA states are party to the international treaties.

Copyright duration

Copyright duration in the UK for works from the UK, EEA, or other countries will not change from 1 January 2021. References to the EEA have been removed from UK law in this area, which means that the duration for EEA works is calculated in the same way as for non-EEA works. However, as copyright duration is equal across the UK and the EEA, there will be no immediate impact on copyright duration in the UK.

****

Ch. 10

Infringement of Copyright

Section 16(1) and (2) Copyright, Designs and Patents Act 1988 states:

"The owner of the copyright in a work has the exclusive right to copy, issue copies of the work, rent, lend, perform, show, play or communicate the work to the public or do any of the above in relation to an adaptation. Copyright in a work is infringed by a person who without the licence of the copyright owner does, or authorises another to do, any of the acts restricted by copyright".

However, the 1988 Act has been significantly amended by a series of Regulations introduced in June 2014 These changes affect infringement of copyright.

Amendments to Copyright law-New Regulations from 2014

The following Regulations have all been brought into force 1st June 2014 and have served to amend the Copyright, Designs and Patents Act 1988.

The Public Administration, Disability, and Research, Education, Libraries and Archives statutory instruments were approved by parliament on 14 May and came into force on 1 June 2014. These instruments will amend relevant sections of the Copyright, Designs and Patents Act 1988.

- The Copyright and Rights in Performances (Disability) Regulations 2014
- The Copyright and Rights in Performances (Personal Copies for Private Use) Regulations 2014
- The Copyright and Rights in Performances (Research, Education, Libraries and Archives) Regulations 2014
- The Copyright (Public Administrations) Regulations 2014
- The Copyright and Rights in Performances (Quotation and Parody) Regulations 2014

Exceptions to copyright

Copyright protects literary, dramatic, musical and artistic works as well as films, sound recordings, book layouts, and broadcasts. If you want to copy or use a copyright work then you usually have to get permission from the copyright owner, but there are a few exceptions where you can copy or use part or all of a copyright work without permission. Where a work contains a performance, the performance will also have rights over how the work is used. The exceptions to copyright also apply to these related rights.

The law on these exceptions has changed in a number of small but important ways, to make the UK copyright system better suited to the digital age. These changes affect how you can use content like books, music, films and photographs.

Personal copies for private use

Copyright law has been changed to allow you to make personal copies of media (ebooks, digital music or video files etc) you have bought, for private purposes such as format shifting or backup. Before this change to the law, it was not legal to copy music that you bought on a CD onto your MP3 player. The changes, which apply from 1 October, update copyright law to make this legal, as long as you own what you are copying, e.g. a music album, and the copy you make is for your own private use.

You are also able to copy a book or film you have bought for one of your devices onto another of your devices, without infringing copyright. However, you should note that media, such as DVDs and e-books, can still be protected by technology which physically prevents copying and circumvention of such technology remains illegal. It is still illegal to make copies for friends or family, or to make a copy of something you do not own or have acquired illegally, without the copyright owner's permission. So you cannot make copies of CDs for your friends, copy CDs borrowed from friends, or copy videos illegally downloaded from file-sharing websites.

The law allows you to make personal copies to any device that you own, or a personal online storage medium, such as a private cloud. However, it is illegal to give other people access to the copies you have made, including, for example, by allowing a friend to access your personal cloud storage.

The exception applies to any copies you have bought, other than computer programs. So, for example, it allows you to format shift an ebook you have bought from one device to another for your own private use. However, you should note that media, such as DVDs and e-books, can still be protected by technology which physically prevents copying and circumvention of such technology remains illegal.

Quotation

Previously, it was an infringement of copyright to take a quotation from one work and use it in another without

138

permission from the copyright owner, unless it was done for the purpose of criticism, review or news reporting.

Copyright law allows quotations to be used more widely without infringing copyright, as long as the use is fair (in law, the use must be a "fair dealing", see the box below) and there is a sufficient acknowledgement - which generally means the title and the author's name should be indicated. It is ultimately for the courts to determine whether use of a quotation is fair dealing, which will depend on the facts of any specific case. However, the use of a title and short extract from a book in an academic article discussing the book is likely to be permitted, whereas the copying of a long extract from a book, without it being justified by the context, is unlikely to be permitted. You may benefit from this law if you are an author, academic, or even just a casual blogger.

Caricature, parody or pastiche

Previously, anyone wishing to use other people's copyright material for the purposes of caricature, parody or pastiche (such as a parody song or video), required the permission of the rights holder. Copyright law now allows limited uses of copyright material for the purposes of caricature, parody or pastiche, without having to obtain the permission of the rights holder. It is important to ensure you understand the limits if you plan to use other people's material for caricature, parody or pastiche. Only minor uses are permitted and a use must be considered fair and reasonable (in law, the use must be a "fair dealing", see the box below), otherwise you must seek permission from the rights holder.

This exception to copyright has no impact on the law of libel or slander, so you may still be sued if a parody work is defamatory.

It also does not affect an author's moral right to object to "derogatory treatment" of their work (as defined in copyright law).

What is fair dealing?

'Fair dealing' is a legal term used to establish whether a use of copyright material is lawful or whether it infringes copyright. There is no statutory definition of fair dealing - it will always be a matter of fact, degree and impression in each case. The question to be asked is: how would a fair-minded and honest person have dealt with the work?

Factors that have been identified by the courts as relevant in determining whether a particular dealing with a work is fair, include:

- Does using the work affect the market for the original work? If a use of a work acts as a substitute for it, causing the owner to lose revenue, then it is not likely to be fair.
- Is the amount of the work taken reasonable and appropriate? Was it necessary to use the amount taken? Usually only part of a work may be used.

The relative importance of any one factor will vary according to the case in hand and the type of dealing in question.

Education and teaching

Changes have been made to copyright law in order to help teachers to deliver modern multi-media teaching without risk of copyright infringement.

The exceptions relating specifically to educational establishments have widened, allowing more extensive use of materials in conjunction with educational licensing schemes.

Another change permits minor acts of copying for teaching purposes, as long as the use is considered fair and reasonable. So, teachers will be able to do things like displaying webpages or quotes on interactive whiteboards, without having to seek additional permission. Education and Teaching

What has changed?

Many schools, colleges and universities copy media which is protected by copyright - for instance photocopying extracts from books for class handouts or recording television programmes to show to a class.

In order to do this, educational establishments hold educational copying licences. So if a school wants to record television broadcasts, it needs a licence from the Educational Recording Agency. If it wants to photocopy extracts from books, it needs a licence from the Copyright Licensing Agency. Most educational establishments already hold these licences.

These licensing schemes are underpinned by copyright exceptions which mean that, where a particular work is not covered by a licence, an educational establishment is still able to copy it. This means that teachers do not have to check the terms of each item they want to copy before they copy it.

The changes to the law apply these exceptions to a wider range of copyright works which were previously not covered - such as artistic works (including photographs), films and sound recordings. They also permit sharing of copies over secure distance learning networks. In order to carry out these activities, schools, colleges and universities simply need to make sure they hold the relevant licences.

The previous law also allowed limited copying of literary, dramatic, musical or artistic works for the purposes of teaching, provided it was not by means of a reprographic process. This meant copying by hand was permitted, but the use of laptops and interactive whiteboards was not. The previous law has been replaced with a general "fair dealing" exception, allowing copying of works in any medium as long as the following conditions apply:

1. the work must be used solely to illustrate a point;
2. the use of the work must not be for commercial purposes;
3. the use must be fair dealing; and
4. it must be accompanied by a sufficient acknowledgement.

This means minor uses, such as displaying a few lines of poetry on an interactive whiteboard, are permitted, but uses which would undermine sales of teaching materials still need a licence. The new law does not remove the need for educational establishments to hold licences for use that does not fall under the "fair dealing" exception, for instance, photocopying material to distribute to students. Schools, colleges and universities still have to pay for third party teaching materials which are available under licence.

Teaching use which is fair dealing, illustrative and non-commercial is permitted by the exception and uses for exam purposes may fall within these criteria. You may also be able to rely on the new quotation exception, for example where you wish to reproduce a piece of text for analysis in an English exam. This would not extend to the making of a reprographic copy of a musical work for use by an examination candidate when performing the work.

Research

The change in the law means that for the first time, researchers and students who need to copy parts of sound recordings, films or broadcasts for non-commercial research or private study are allowed to do so. Libraries and archives are also able to make copies of artistic works for researchers and students. Education institutions, libraries, archives and museums are able to offer access to copyright works on their premises by electronic means at dedicated terminals.

Researchers and students were previously allowed to copy limited extracts of literary, dramatic, musical and artistic works for non-commercial research and private study. They are now able to copy a limited amount of a sound recording, film or broadcast. This amount is restricted by fair dealing, which rules out unfair or unreasonable uses such as copying a whole film for "research" instead of buying the DVD. Any use made of the work must be accompanied by a sufficient acknowledgement.

Quotation

What has changed? Before the law changed, minor uses of quotations from copyright works could be prevented by copyright owners, unless they fell within fair dealing exceptions for criticism, review or news reporting.

The law has been amended to give people greater freedom to quote the works of others for other purposes, as long as this is reasonable and fair ("fair dealing").

Caricature, parody or pastiche

The ability to re-edit copyright works in new and experimental ways is seen as an important learning and teaching exercise for creative skills.

Many works of caricature, parody or pastiche, involve some level of copying from another work. The law has changed to allow limited uses of other people's copyright material for the purposes of caricature, parody or pastiche, without first asking for permission.

Changes affecting disabled people

The Government has made it easier for disabled people to access materials that are protected by copyright. Previously there were exceptions to copyright law that allowed visually-impaired people, and organisations acting on their behalf, to make accessible versions (e.g. Braille versions) of certain types of material, such as books. Also, the law allowed certain designated organisations to produce sub-titled copies of broadcasts for people who are deaf or hard of hearing.

However, these exceptions did not apply to other types of impairment, such as dyslexia, and did not apply to all types of copyright work. The law has changed so that anyone who has an impairment that prevents them accessing copyright works will now be able to benefit from the exception, not just visually-impaired people. The law also allows individuals, educational establishments and not-for-profit organisations to reproduce all types of copyright-protected content in accessible formats.

These changes will give disabled people greater access to creative content, as individuals, educational establishments and charities are allowed to reproduce material without purchasing a licence as long as a copy is not already commercially available in an accessible format.

Also, the law has been simplified so that organisations wishing to produce sub-titled copies of broadcasts on behalf of

144

deaf and other disabled people will be able to do so without going through a bureaucratic designation process.

What's allowed?
The change in the law makes the rules on what can be copied into an accessible format much broader so that a whole range of content, including films and broadcasts, can be reproduced in an accessible format for disabled people.

The law allows acts such as:

- Making Braille, audio or large-print copies of books, newspapers or magazines for visually-impaired people
- Adding audio-description to films or broadcasts for visually-impaired people
- Making sub-titled films or broadcasts for deaf or hard of hearing people
- Making accessible copies of books, newspapers or magazines for dyslexic people

However, it is only legal to reproduce material if suitable accessible copies are not commercially available. Organisations that make and supply accessible-format copies for disabled people have a duty to keep records of the copies they make and provide them to the copyright owner of the material.

Research
What's changed? The law already permitted limited copying of some types of copyright material, such as books, for non-commercial research or genuine private study. The law has now changed so that all types of copyright works are covered.

Text and data mining technologies help researchers process large amounts of data.

Copyright law has altered to help ensure that if a researcher is carrying out non-commercial research they will not infringe copyright by copying material for a text and data mining analysis. The conditions under which this exception applies are set out in this guidance.

Copying works for research and private study

Copyright law recognises that researchers and students may legitimately need to copy limited extracts of copyright works for the purpose of their studies. Therefore, the law already allowed researchers and students to copy limited extracts of some types of copyright works (books, plays and musical scores, picture and photos, literary, dramatic musical and artistic works) as long as they are carrying out non-commercial research or private study. Librarians are permitted to assist researchers and students by providing limited copies of these types of copyright works.

What has changed?

Copyright law has now changed so that all types of published copyright works are covered by the exception allowing limited copying for the purpose of research. This means that researchers and students (or the librarians and archivists who are assisting them) who need to copy limited parts of sound recordings, films or broadcasts for non-commercial research or private study are allowed to do so. The provisions about only copying a part of a work and sufficiently acknowledging the original work still apply.

Additionally, educational institutions, libraries, archives and museums are now permitted to offer access to copyright works on their premises at dedicated electronic terminals for research and private study. More information can be found in the leaflet "Exceptions to copyright: Libraries, archives and museums".

Text and Data Mining for non-commercial research

Text and data mining is the use of automated analytical techniques to analyse text and data for patterns, trends and other useful information. Text and data mining usually requires copying of the work to be analysed. Before the law was changed, researchers using text and data mining in their research risked infringing copyright unless they had specific permission from the copyright owner.

The new copyright exception allows researchers to make copies of any copyright material for the purpose of computational analysis if they already have the right to read the work (that is, work that they have "lawful access" to). They will be able to do this without having to obtain permission to make copies from the rights holder. This exception only permits the making of copies for the purpose of text and data mining for non-commercial research. Researchers will still have to buy subscriptions to access material; this could be from many sources including academic publishers.

Publishers and content providers are able to apply reasonable measures to maintain their network security or stability so long as these measures do not prevent or unreasonable restrict a researcher's ability to make the copies they need to make for their text and data mining. Contract terms that stop researchers making copies of works to which they have lawful access in order to carry out a text and data mining analysis will be unenforceable.

Quotation

Before the law changed, minor uses of quotations from copyright works could be prevented by copyright owners, unless they fell within fair dealing exceptions for criticism, review or news reporting.

The law has been amended to give people greater freedom to quote the works of others for other purposes, as long as this is reasonable and fair ("fair dealing).

Copyright material held by public bodies

Some material held by public bodies will have been submitted by third parties, such as by members of the public, businesses or researchers. For example this could be material submitted to a public body, such as local authority, as part of a duty to capture information required for public register.

Where a public body holds third party material - that is, material in which someone other than the public body owns the copyright - the general position has been that an individual could either view that material in person, or a public body could copy and distribute it on an individual basis. The law did not generally allow such material to be published online without permission from the rights holders.

Public bodies and keepers of statutory registers are now allowed to proactively share copyright material online without seeking permission, as long as it is not commercially available. The same applies to material that is already available for public inspection through some statutory mechanism, such as local planning applications.

This change does not permit public bodies to publish material that is commercially available to buy or license (such as academic articles). In these circumstances any public body would still need to seek the permission of the rights holder.

Another change in this area applies to certain works that have been communicated to the Crown with the permission of the copyright owner and in the course of public business. This exception applies only to literary, dramatic, musical or artistic works that have not previously been published.

The change to the law will make it easier for the public to access information, saving both time and expense for public bodies and individuals.

Libraries, Museums and Archives

The law has changed to make it easier and cheaper for cultural institutions like libraries, archives, and museums to use, share and preserve their collections.

There are two significant changes which will affect libraries, archives and museums. The first relates to making copies of works to preserve them for future generations. The second allows greater freedom to copy works for those carrying out non-commercial research and private study.

Archiving and preservation of resources

Changes to copyright law for archiving and preservation will make it easier to preserve creative content held by libraries, archives and museums. These institutions are now allowed to preserve any type of copyright work that is held in their permanent collection (but not available for loan to the public) and cannot readily be replaced.

There is a risk that both the original and the copy of a work may degenerate or corrupt over time. Making a single copy may be insufficient to safeguard a work in the long term.

Research and private study

Copying works for research and private study

Librarians are permitted to assist researchers and students by providing limited copies of books, plays and musical scores, pictures and photos, literary, dramatic, musical and artistic works for non-commercial research and private study. The amount that can be copied is restricted to a reasonable proportion. This rules out unfair or unreasonable uses such as copying a whole film for "research" instead of buying the DVD and generally means that only a part of a work can be copied. Use made of the work should be accompanied by sufficient acknowledgement (e.g. in a reference or bibliography).

What's changed?

The law has changed so that all types of published copyright works are now covered by the provisions in copyright law allowing limited copying for non-commercial research and private study. The same provisions about only copying a part of a work and sufficiently acknowledging the author still apply.

Educational institutions, libraries, archives and museums are now permitted to offer access to copyright works on their premises at dedicated electronic terminals for research and private study.

How does a librarian ensure that the person is genuinely doing non-commercial research or private study?

A librarian who is supplying a copy of a work will wish to ask a researcher to declare that they are doing non-commercial research, this can now be done electronically`(for example, an electronic copyright declaration form could be signed using a typed signature or check-box).

What types of libraries are able to provide copies of work?
Publicly accessible libraries and archives, such as those run by universities, schools, local council, government departments and NHS institutions can provide copies of copyright work for non-commercial research and private study, as set out in this guidance. The provisions do not extend to private libraries or archives, such as law firms that run on a commercial basis.

Libraries, archives and museums
How much of a work is a librarian allowed to copy for a student or researcher?

The amount you are able to copy of a published work is limited to a reasonable proportion, and a copyright declaration must be provided. This generally means that only a limited part that is necessary for the research project may be copied.

However, archivists may supply a single copy of a whole or part of a work provided that the work had not been published or communicated before it was deposited in the library or archive, or the owner of that work has not prohibited the copying of that work. As usual, a copyright declaration must be provided.

Defences to Copyright infringement
There are a number of defences to infringement:
a) Challenge the existence of copyright or the claimant's ownership of copyright.
b) Deny the infringement.
c) Claim to have been entitled, because of permission granted to do the act in question or argue that it is within one of the statutory fair dealing exemptions or by claiming public interest or EC competition rights.

A claim of ignorance of the law will not work as a defence. Ignorance of subsistence of copyright will, however, have a bearing on any damages awarded. In the case of secondary infringement an element of knowledge is required for the infringement to be actionable in the first place. The infringement only occurs if the person knows that what he or she is dealing with is an infringing copyright work.

If the claimant does own copyright in the work that is allegedly infringed, and facts can be proved, the only defences remaining are:

1) that the defendant had permission from the copyright owner to make a copy.

Provided that the defendant in an infringement action can prove that permission was granted, either in writing, orally or, in certain cases, implied, then the claim of infringement will fail.

2) That the act was one of the permitted acts under the 1988 Act, as amended

The 1988 Act, as amended, contains statutory permissions, or exceptions, to the exclusive rights of the copyright owner. Many of these have come from the results of case decisions over the years that have acknowledged the need for fair exceptions. These permitted acts are categorised in the Act and comprise:

- Research and private study
- Criticism review and news reporting
- Incidental inclusion of copyright material
- Things done for instruction or examination

- Anthologies for educational use
- Playing, showing or performing in an educational establishment
- Recordings by educational establishments
- Reprographic copying by educational establishments
- Libraries and archives
- Public administration
- Lawful users of computer programs and databases
- DesignsTypefaces
- Works in electronic form

All of the above are categorised in the Act and each case concerning these categories will be on its own merit.

3) That the exercise of the copyright owner's rights to prevent copying would amount to an anti-competitive practice under EC competition law.

4) That the exercise of the copyright owner's rights is against the public interest.

Each one of the above must be proven and each case will be judged on its own merit.

****

Ch. 11

Design Law

Design law and BREXIT

There will be key changes to Design Law after Britain's exit from the EU (with effect from January 1st 2020, affecting unregistered designs and the applications to register designs. There is a summary of these changes at the end of this chapter.

Design

A design may be protected in a number of ways, in particular by the Community Design, (Registered Design and Unregistered Design) the UK Registered Design and the UK Unregistered Design Right. The UK Registered and unregistered design rights have been amended by the introduction of the Intellectual Property Act 2014 which came into force between October 2014 and the end of 2015. This is outlined at the end of this chapter.

Community Design

There are two forms of Community design, one subject to registration (RCD) and the other informal (UCD). The basic requirements are both the same, apart from the date at which novelty and individual character is tested.

A community design has a unitary character and has equal effect throughout the Community. It may only be registered, transferred, surrendered, declared invalid or its use prohibited in relation to the entire community.

The main legislation dealing with community design is Article 3 Community Design regulation OJ 2002 L341:

a) 'design' means the appearance of the whole or part of a product resulting from the features of, in particular, the lines, contours, colours, shape, texture and/or materials of the product itself and /or its ornamentation;

b) 'product means any industrial or handicraft item, including *inter alia* parts intended to be assembled into a complex product, packaging, get up, graphic, symbols and typographic typefaces but excluding computer programs:

c) 'complex product' means a product which is composed of multiple components which can be replaced, permitting disassembly and re-assembly of the product.

Article 4 (1) Community Design regulation

A design shall be protected by a community design to the extent that it is new and has individual character.

Novelty and Individual character

A design is new if no identical design (including a design with features which differ only in immaterial details) has been made available to the public. There is a proviso to this and that is a pre-existing design will be disregarded if it could not reasonably have become known in the normal course of business to the circles specialized in the sector concerned operating in the community.

A design has an individual character if the overall impression it produces on an informed user differs from the overall impression produced on such a user by any design which has been made available to the public.

A key case concerning novelty and individual character is that of Green Lane Products Ltd v PMS International Group Ltd (2008). In this case, a challenge to the validity of the claimant's Community design for spiky laundry balls was based on the defendant's similar shaped spiky balls used for massaging the human body.

It was established in this case that the prior art is not limited to the particular product for which the design was registered, as the scope of infringement is not limited to the product for which it was intended to apply the design. For example, the registration of a design intended for motor cars would protect also against its use for toys. The 'informed user' is not the same as the average consumer of trade mark law. The informed user has experience of similar products and will be reasonably discriminatory and able to appreciate sufficient detail to decide whether or not the design under consideration creates a different overall impression. The degree of design freedom is taken into account.

A key case concerning individual character and design freedom is that of Pepsico Inc's design (No ICD000000172) OHIM.

The design in question was for a disk having annular rings or corrugations applied to a promotional item for games. There was a challenge to the validity of the design. The design was declared invalid.

The legal principle was that the informed consumer would be familiar with promotional items and would pay more attention to graphical elements rather than minor variations in shape. Furthermore, although there were some constraints to design freedom, these were to do with cost and safety, and, otherwise, there was ample design freedom. Thus, the informed user may focus on certain aspects of a design and design freedom should be looked at in the round and some constraints may be present without significantly reducing the overall design freedom.

Time periods for testing novelty and individual character

The time when a design has been made available to the public differs between the RCD and the UCD (Registered and Unregistered). The RCD relevant date is the date of filing the application, or earlier priority date if there is one. The UCD relevant date is the date the design itself is first made available to the public.

There is a 12-month period of grace for the RCD so, for example the designer may market products relating to that design during that period before filing the application to register. "Under the bonnet' parts which are not seen during normal use of a complex product are not considered to be novel or have individual character.

Exclusions from Community Design

The below are exclusions from community design:

- Features dictated by technical function
- 'Must-fit' features (except in respect of modular systems which are protectable in principle)
- Designs contrary to public policy or morality
- "Must-match' spare parts used to restore the original appearance of a complex product.

Duration

Registered Community Designs – five years from the date of filing. It may then be renewed for further periods of five years up to a maximum of 25 years. Unregistered Community Designs-three years from the date the design was first made available to the public.

For the purpose of the unregistered design in determining the start of the three years, it is made available to the public when it is published, exhibited, used in trade or other wise disclosed in such a way that, in the normal course of the business, these events could have reasonably have become known to the circles specialized in the sector concerned in the community.

Protection and infringement of a community design

The scope of protection of a community design resembles the test for individual character in that it is a question of whether the alleged infringing design, from the perspective of the informed user, does not produce a different overall impression compared with the protected design. Design freedom is taken into consideration.

The main legislation concerning protection of community design is Article 10 Community Design Regulation OJ 2002 L341:

- The scope of protection conferred by a community design shall include any design which does not produce on the informed user a different overall impression.
- In assessing the scope of protection, the degree of freedom of the designer in developing his design shall be taken into consideration.

The registered community design gives the rightholder a monopoly right which is infringed by a person using it without the rightholders consent. Use, in particular, includes making, offering, putting on the market, importing, exporting or using a product in which the design is incorporated or applied, or stocking such a product for those purposes.

For the unregistered Community design, it is required that the use in question results from copying the protected design. This also applies during the period of deferred publication where the design is registered but publication has been deferred. An applicant to register a Community design can defer publication by up to 30 months from the filing date, hence delaying the payment of the publication fee.

A key case concerning infringement was that of Procter and Gamble Co v Reckitt Benckiser (UK) Ltd (2008) which was a case on the alleged infringement of a registered Community design applied to a spray container for air fresheners.

It was found in this case that a design did not have to be clearly different, it was sufficient if it differed in a way that the informed user was able to discriminate. An initial decision that there had been an infringement was reversed.

Limitations on the rights to a Community design

The rights to a Community design (registered or unregistered) do not extend to the following acts:

- Acts done privately and for non-commercial purposes.
- Acts done for experimental purposes
- Reproduction for citation or teaching in accordance with fair practices without unduly prejudicing the normal exploitation of the design, providing the source is mentioned.
- Acts in respect of the repair of ships or aircraft temporarily in the Community.

UK registered design

The UK registered design has been modified as a result of the EU Directive harmonising registered design law throughout the

European Community. As a result, the main principles in the EU and UK are virtually identical.

The main legislation dealing with registered designs in the UK is section 24A (2) of the Registered Designs Act 1949 and Regulation 1A (2) Community Design regulations 2005/2339, as amended. In addition, the Intellectual Property Act 2014 has made changes to both UK registered and unregistered designs as outlined below.

UK unregistered design right

The UK unregistered design right was introduced by the Copyright, Designs and Patents Act 1988 in an attempt to overcome the problems of protection of functional designs by means of copyright in drawings showing the designs, as highlighted in *British Leyland Motor Corp v Armstrong patents Co Ltd (1986).*

The main legislation Section 213(1), (2) and (4) Copyright, Designs and Patents Act 1988, as amended, states:

(1) Design right is a property right which subsists in accordance with this part in an original design.

(2) In this part, 'design' means the design of any aspect of the shape or configuration (whether internal or external) of the whole or part of an article.

(3) A design is not 'original' for the purposes of this part if it is commonplace in the design field in question at the time of its creation.

Exceptions to subsistence of UK unregistered design right

Sections 213 (3) Copyright, Designs and Patents act 1988 states:

(3) Design right does not subsist in -

(a) a method of principle of construction,
(b) features of shape or configuration of an article which -
(i) enable the article to be connected to, or placed in, around or against another article so that either article may perform its function, or
(ii) are dependant upon the appearance of another article of which the article is intended by the designer to form an integral part, or
(c) surface decoration.
The first exception, methods or principles of construction, is unlikely to be relevant in the majority of cases. then other exceptions are often referred to as the 'must fit' or 'must match' exceptions. Surface decoration is also excepted.

A key case in the area is that of Dyson Ltd v Qualtex (UK) Ltd (2006) which concerned various aspects of design right including the scope of the 'must fit' and 'must match' and surface decoration exclusions.

The facts of the case were that the defendant supplied duplicate spare parts (pattern parts) for the claimant's vacuum cleaners. The claimant sued on the basis of the unregistered design rights subsisting in the design of the parts of its vacuum cleaners.

The court found that the 'must fit' exclusion does not mean that the articles have to physically touch. A clearance between them, if it allows one article to perform its function, may be within the exclusion. the exclusion may apply where the two articles are designed sequentially one after the other.

For 'must match' exclusion it is the design dependency which is important. the more room there is for design freedom, the less likely the exception will apply. The reason for the surface decoration exclusion was because it was protected by copyright. Surface decoration could be applied to a two-dimensional article or three dimensional article or to a flat surface of a three dimensional article. Surface decoration was not limited to something applied to an existing article and it could come into existence with the surface itself. Surface decoration could be three dimensional such as beading applied to furniture. However, a feature having a function, such as ribbing on the handle of a vacuum cleaner, was unlikely to be surface decoration.

The Intellectual Property Act 2014
Stemming from the Hargreaves Review on intellectual property reform, the Act seeks to modernise and simplify certain aspects of intellectual property law including the law relating to designs, in order to promote innovation.

What are the purposes of the changes to design rights?
The purpose of the design right changes are to:

- simplify design law and allow the intellectual property framework to better support innovation
- improve the enforcement of designs and understanding the design rights of others, and
- improve the processes associated with the design framework

What changes are made to design right protection?
Unregistered Designs
- Designer is now the first owner: One fundamental change to existing law is that the act changes the deemed first owner

of unregistered designs so that unless otherwise agreed, the designer will be the owner of the designs and not the person who commissioned the designs. Historically the first owner has been the commissioner. This amendment will bring design law into line with UK copyright law

- Trivial design features limited: The definition of Unregistered Design Right has been amended to limit the protection for trivial features of a design

- Clarification of definition of 'design': The act clarifies the definition of design so that to be original a design must not be commonplace in a 'qualifying country' rather than in the 'relevant design field', which caused confusion as to its geographical coverage. Qualifying Country is defined in the Copyright Designs and Patents Act 1988 (CDPA)

- Qualifying Person amended: The act has amended the provisions related to qualifying persons who can claim unregistered design right so that those who are economically active in the EU and other Qualifying Countries (as set out in the CDPA) have protection

- New exceptions to infringement: The act extends the exceptions for infringing unregistered designs, so that acts done privately for no commercial purpose or for teaching will not infringe unregistered design rights. A similar exception applies for acts done for experimental purposes, this is to encourage innovation

Registered Designs

- Designer is now the first owner: The initial ownership position in respect of registered designs is also changed, as for unregistered designs i.e. the designer will be the initial owner unless otherwise agreed, rather than the commissioner.

- New Criminal Offence: The act makes intentional copying of a registered design a criminal offence. This applies to acts which take place in the course of business and the penalties for such an offence are now a fine or prison sentence. Again, this brings the penalties into line with sanctions for trade marks and copyright infringement.

- New exceptions to infringement: The act expands the exception from copyright infringement already available to registered UK designs to registered community designs, i.e. so that an authorised user of a UK or registered community design cannot be sued for infringement of associated copyright.

- Applicant does not need to be the owner of the design: The act removes the requirement for the applicant of a registered design application to be the proprietor of the design.

- New good faith exception to infringement: The act introduces a right of prior use, allowing a third party who has acted in good faith to continue to use a registered design which is subsequently registered by another. The aim of this amendment is to provide an entitlement to limited exploitation in respect of uses already made.

- New powers of enforcement: The act gives Trading Standards officers similar powers of enforcement for design offences as those already available to them in respect of copyright and trade marks.

- Simplified international registration: The act grants power for the Secretary of State to implement the Geneva Act of the Hague Agreement in the UK, this means that international registration procedures will be available for UK registered designs. At present UK designers can only access the Hague registration process via the EU community design registration.

- Harmonisation of financial liability: The act aligns the financial liability provisions for innocent infringement with those provisions under the Community Design Rights legislation.

- Simplified appeal process: The act allows a new route of appeal against Intellectual Property Office (IPO) decisions via an Appointed Person instead of appealing via the courts, such root already exist for trade mark appeals. This amendment is intended to allow appeals be cheaper and less time consuming.

- New opinions service for ownership, validity and infringement issues: The act provides for a voluntary non-binding opinion service to be introduced by the IPO which is similar to the opinions service which currently exists in respect of patents.

- Clarification: The act clarifies that proceedings for an offence committed against a partnership must be brought against the partnership.

- derived from a continuing programme of research, a report of which is intended for future publication, where disclosure would prejudice the report.

Changes to Design Law after January 1st 2020

After the end of the Transition Period, at 11.00 pm on 31 December 2020 those who currently own protection for designs in the UK need to understand how things will change for them going forward. In particular, they need to understand how protection in the UK based on EU rights up until Completion Day will continue from 1 January 2021, and what strategies they need to adopt for new designs going forwards, and in particular where they should first disclose them. The key points are as follows:

- UK registered designs will continue as they are and will be unaffected by Brexit;

- Registered Community designs, which until Completion Day will protect the design in question in the UK, will no longer do so from 1 January 2021. However, a comparable UK registered design will be entered into the UK designs register automatically, and at no cost, effective from Completion Day. It will have the same scope and filing and registration date as the earlier registered Community design;

- If a registered Community design application is pending on Completion Day, the applicant will have 9 months from Completion Day to make an application for the same design in the UK, and will be able to rely on the registered Community design application's filing or priority date;

- If registered design protection is required in the UK and the EU from 1 January 2021, it will be necessary to apply separately for protection in both;

- Unregistered UK design right, which protects the original shape and configuration (but not the surface decoration) of articles in the UK from being copied, usually for a period of

10 years from when the article is first made available for sale, will also remain largely unaffected by Brexit;

- Unregistered Community designs, however, which protect aspects of a design different to those protected by UK unregistered design right from being copied, including 2 dimensional surface decoration, as well as 3 dimensional aspects of the contours and shape of a product, will no longer provide protection in the UK after completion day;

- To provide the same protection in the UK as was provided here by unregistered Community designs before Completion Day, two new rights will be created. Firstly, for an unregistered Community design in existence on IP Completion Day, a "continuing unregistered design" will arise automatically in the UK on Completion Day, providing the same scope of protection in the UK as was previously provided under the unregistered Community design, and which will expire when the corresponding unregistered Community design expires;

- Secondly, a "supplementary unregistered design" will also be created in the UK, which will sit alongside the UK unregistered design right, and provide the same protection which, were it not for Brexit, would have been provided by an unregistered Community design here;

- People in the UK will still be able to secure protection for their designs in the EU under an unregistered Community design after Completion Day, but a very important question is whether this will only be available if the design in question is first made available to the public (e.g. at a trade show) in the EU, which many practitioners believe the law currently requires.

From 1 January 2021, if a UK designer first makes a design available in the UK, that will no longer satisfy the "first make available in the EU" test, this is likely to deprive them of EU wide unregistered design protection. They will secure protection in the UK, as first making the design available in the UK will be a requirement to obtaining the supplementary unregistered design here, but the UK has made clear that this UK right will not be available to designs first made available to the public in the EU after 1 January 2021.

So those who do business in both the UK and some or all of the 27 EU member states, are likely to have to choose between first making their designs available and securing protection here, or first making their designs available and securing protection in the EU. They are unlikely to be able to secure this form of protection in both, unless first making the design available via the internet on web pages which are targeted at both the UK and the EU, is determined by the courts or recognised in legislation as constituting a simultaneous first making of the design available in both the UK and the EU. Until this occurs, and if protection is required in both the EU and the UK, then the safest course will be to register the design in whichever of the two locations the design was not first made available.

****

Ch. 12

Applying for a Registered Design

You can apply for Registered Design protection by filling out the appropriate application form(s), found on the IPO website, and paying the relevant fee.

Design application form DF2A

This is the most commonly used form. It is essential that you refer to DF2A notes and the 'How to apply to register a design' booklet for instructions on how to complete the form.

Surplus design application form DF2B

Use this form if the IPO has asked you to divide out a design from an earlier application.

Refer to DF2A and DF2B notes for guidance on how to complete the form, and also the 'How to apply to register a design' booklet (536Kb) for instructions on filling out the form.

You will need to send new copies of your representations for any designs on the DF2B *and* the design remaining on the original application.

Send the application

You should send your application to the IPO. You must include your completed DF2A and fee sheet forms, one copy of the illustrations of your design, and your fee. It is not advised to fax design applications as the loss of detail on your representations may affect the amount of protection you have, and you may lose your filing date if the IPO have to ask for better images.

How much does it cost?
If you wish to have your design or designs published and registered as soon as possible:

- It costs GBP £50 to apply to register a single design (Online 2019) or £60 paper application, or the first design in any multiple application. For more than one it costs:

  - Up to 10 • £70
  - Up to 20 • £90
  - Up to 30 • £110
  - Up to 40 • £130
  - Up to 50 • £150

- If you wish to defer the publication of a design by up to 12 months:
- It costs GBP £40 to apply and to register a single design or the first design in any multiple application.For every additional design in a multiple application it costs GBP £20 per design.
- When you are ready to request publication and registration of deferred designs you will need to file Form DF2C and pay a publication fee of GBP £40 per design.

For more details of fees go to

https://www.gov.uk/government/publications/design-forms-and-fees/design-forms-and-fees

Why might I need to defer publication?

If you are applying for a patent or wish to delay the public disclosure of the design for any reason, you may wish to defer registration and publication of your design.

Changing or renewing your registered design

You can change or renew the details of your registered design in various ways.

Changing
Appoint or change an agent or contact details

You can appoint a specialist attorney, to deal with your application or some complicated part of the procedures for you.

Cancelling your design

You can cancel your own design registration at any time. The implications of cancellation are quite far-reaching.

Renewing-Renewing your design

To keep your registered design in force, you must renew it on the 5th anniversary of the registration date and every 5 years after that up to a total of 25 years.

Restoration

If you registered your design on or after 1 August 1989 and you do not renew it in the 6 months after the renewal date, you have a further 6 months, to apply to restore your registration.

Appointing or changing an agent or contact address

You can use DF1A to remove or appoint a person, company or agent to deal with your application or any other complicated part of our procedures for you. It can also be used to alter the contact details that the IPO hold for you.There is no fee for this.

What happens next?
The IPO will record the change or appointment and send written confirmation to you.

Correcting an error
You can correct an error in your design in the following ways:
 amending the details on your application form (except name and address); or
• amending errors in the illustrations of your design; or
• amending your entry in the register of designs

Errors can usually only be corrected following a clerical or obvious error. You will need to write to the IPO with your request. There is no fee for this. You should use the IPO Proprietor Search to make sure you have listed all the Designs affected. Send your request to:

What happens next?
The IPO will consider the request and, if acceptable, will record it on the Designs Register and send written confirmation to you.

Cancelling your registered design
You can cancel your design registration at any time. This action is usually taken

• to avoid legal action such as infringement proceedings; or
• because of an application to remove the registered design by a third party

You will need to make sure you are aware of any implications of cancelling your design, for example if you have licensed the design to someone based on your registration. To cancel your own registration, fill in form DF19C There is no charge for this.

What happens next?
The IPO will cancel the registration and write to confirm that they have done so.

Renewing your design
To keep your registered design in force, you must renew it on the 5th anniversary of the registration date and every 5 years after that.

You can renew your design up for 25 years, but you may choose not to renew it or to voluntarily cancel it at any time. You can renew your registration up to 6 months before the renewal date. The IPO will write to remind you 3 months before renewal is due if you have not already renewed it.

How do I renew my registered design?
To extend the period of protection, fill in form **DF9A** and **FS2** and send the correct fee. The renewal fees are as follows: (2021)

Period	Fee
1st	£70
2nd	£90
3rd	£110
4th	£140
Late renewal (additional fee)	£24 per month
Restore a design	£120

What happens next?

The IPO will write to confirm that they have renewed your design for the next 5-year period.

What if I don't renew in time?

If you do not pay your renewal fee by the renewal date your registration becomes expired. The IPO will write to confirm this, but you can still renew it within 1 month of the renewal date at no extra charge. You have a further 5 months in which to renew your design. However, there is a late payment fee of £24 for each of these months in addition to the renewal fee. If you do not renew your design within this 6 month period you can still apply to restore your design.

Restoring your design

After the 6-month late renewal period, there is a further 6 month period where you can apply to restore your design.

Restoration

If you registered your design on or after 1 August 1989 and you do not renew it in the 6 months after the renewal date, you have a further 6 months, to apply to restore your registration.

You cannot restore designs registered before 1 August 1989 that have not been renewed within the 6 months, allowed.

Fill in Form DF29

To restore a registered design, complete and submit Form DF29 enclosing the following:

- a statement of the reasons for your failure to renew, and
- a fee of GBP £120

What happens next?

the IPO will process your application to consider restoration of registered designs and give notice of the application in the Designs Journal. If they are satisfied that failure to pay the renewal fee was unintentional, they will write to tell you and ask you to send them:

- Form DF9A - Application to extent the period of protection and
- The correct renewal fee

Once they receive your forms and fees, they will restore your design to the register and publish that fact in the Designs Journal. If they are not satisfied that your failure to renew was unintentional, they will:

- write and explain why they have not accepted your reasons; and
- allow you 2 months to request a hearing.

If you do not request a hearing within 2 months, they will refuse your application and publish that fact in the DesigJournal.ns

Using and enforcing your design

You can decide how to use and enforce your registered design.

Using-Licensing and selling

You can give someone else permission to use your Registered Design by granting them a licence, or you can sell (assign) it.

Mortgaging

You can use your registered design as security for a loan. The mortgagor has a legal right in your design until you repay the loan.

Marketing

You may want to involve others to help exploit, develop or market your design.

Enforcing your design

Display your rights

There is no official symbol to show that a design is registered but you can display the design number on the product once it is registered.

The IPO always encourage parties who are in dispute to resolve their differences before seeking a judgment by them, but they do offer a mediation service which may help.

Certified and uncertified copies

The IPO will supply a copy of a design or design application, upon request and payment of a fee.

Licensing

You can give someone else permission to use your registered design by granting them a licence.The terms of any licence are entirely a matter between you and the licensee. You or the licensee should register the licence, or cancellation of a licence, with the IPO and they will record it in the register of designs.

Licensing of unregistered rights

The IPO offers some limited services in relation to licensing of unregistered Design Right.

Display your rights

There is no official symbol to show that a design is registered, but you can display the design number on the product once it is registered.

However, please note, under Section 35 of the Registered Designs Act 1949 as amended it is an offence to falsely claim that a design is registered.

Your design registration is not valid until the IPO have issued your certificate, so it is still an offence to claim your design is registered during the period of time in between applying for a registration and receiving confirmation from the IPO that registration has been granted. This includes applications which have been deemed acceptable but for which deferred registration and publication has been requested.

During this period, you can state that design registration has been applied for, but not that it has been granted.

Before proceedings commence

Lord Woolf's 1986 report 'Access to Justice' identified the need for parties to see legal action as a last resort. He suggested that they should first try to settle matters outside the judicial system. This is the same approach as adopted with all disputes connected to Intellectual property. In the first instance, try to resolve the matter before action. These principles are reflected in the Civil Procedure Rules which were introduced in April 1999. In line with those Rules, if an action is launched before the Registrar and there is no prior contact between the parties, they

177

may be penalised when the costs of the case are determined. So if you are thinking of taking legal action you should attempt to resolve the matter before launching any action.

Mediation

Mediation is another route that the IPO will be actively encouraging. It is another way that parties can resolve their dispute.

Requests for stays or suspensions in inter partes proceedings

Where a stay or suspension is requested because the parties are trying to negotiate an amicable settlement, the parties will need to show what they have already done to resolve the dispute. If the IPO is not satisfied that those negotiations are making progress they will not allow any further extensions to the stay of proceedings.

Hearing or written decision

When any period allowed for the filing of evidence is over the IPO will offer the parties either a hearing or a decision from the papers already filed. In either case the IPO decision will resolve the dispute. The decision will be open to appeal.

Certified and uncertified copies

The IPO will supply a copy of a design or design application, upon request and payment of the relevant fee. You can also access the register on-line and get designs information free of charge.

You can request copies as filed, or as registered. Copies of applications which have not yet been registered may only be issued to the applicant or their agent.

- **Certified copies (Certificates of the Registrar)** give proof that the United Kingdom Designs Registry has received an application to register or has granted registration of a design, in accordance with the Registered Designs Act and Rules, and that that copy was formally issued by the Intellectual Property Office.
- **Uncertified copies** are photocopied documents.

What type of copy do I need?
You must use certified copies:
- When needed as evidence in a court of law, for example if you are involved in legal action to enforce or defend your design rights. You may also need to use certified copies:
- When applying for a design abroad and claiming a Priority Date from your earlier UK application.

You can use uncertified copies for your personal reference or research.

Costs and how to pay
- A Certificate of the Registrar costs £22.
- A photocopy (uncertified) costs £5 per file copied which includes postage, though the IPO reserve the right to quote for their actual costs where particularly large files are involved.
- A fee sheet must be filed with all fee bearing forms.

To request a certified copy
- Use form DF23 Request for a certified copy.

- Use a separate form for each design or design application.
- Send your completed form DF23, FS2 fee sheet and payment to the IPO

To request an uncertified copy

- E-mail the IPO at sales@ipo.gov.uk
- Phone the IPO on 0300 300 2000.
- Fax the IPO on 01633 817777.

Selling your design
You are free to sell or transfer ownership of your registered design to someone else. If you do, you must tell the IPO so they can record the change in the register of designs. This includes any change of ownership as a result of company mergers. The legal term for a transfer of ownership is an assignment.

Fill in Form DF12A
To tell the IPO you have sold your registered design you need to fill in form DF12A . There is no charge for this. Form DF12A is not a replacement for the assignment, merely the form that you should use to ask the IPO to record it.

You and the new owners or their representatives must sign the form. If any of them cannot do so, the IPO will accept other documents as proof that the assignment has taken place.

What happens next?
The IPO will record the details of the assignment in the register of designs and write to confirm that they have done so

Designs protection abroad

Registering your design in the UK does not protect it abroad.

If you want to register your design in countries other than the UK, there are a number of ways in which you can do so.

- You can apply for a Registered Community Design (RCD) covering the whole of the European Union ('EU'). However, note that this changes in 2021 after BRitains exit from the EU-see a summary of changes at the end of the previous chapter.
- You can apply directly to most major countries of the world by making a separate application to each country in which you want protection.
- You can use the Hague System to apply to a number of different countries or territories at the same time, through a single application.

Using unregistered design rights

You may also be able to rely on automatic copyright and unregistered design rights in the countries concerned, eg. the Unregistered Community Design right (UCD) which covers the whole of the EU. Again, see notes on Brexit in the previous chapter.

Claiming a priority date

If you are applying for a design in another country within 6 months of applying for the same design in the UK, or if you are applying in the UK within 6 months of filing elsewhere in the world, you may be able to have the date on which you applied for the earlier design accepted as the date on which you filed the later application. Priority dates may only be granted in relation to countries which have signed up to the Paris Convention or which are Members of the World Trade Organisation (WTO).

Using the Hague System

The Hague System for the International Registration of Industrial Designs allows you to simultaneously apply for a design in many different countries or territories, through a single application to the World Intellectual Property Organisation (WIPO). An application under the Hague System will cover the UK if the EU is selected.

****

Ch. 13

Intellectual Property and Computer Software

Computer software and computer designs have pushed the boundaries of intellectual property law.

All forms of copyright work can exist in digital form and the Copyright, Designs and Patents Act 1988 acknowledges this, for example, by providing that copying includes copying in electronic form and also extends to transient and temporary copies. protection is also given to technological measures to prevent unauthorised acts in relation to computer programmes (in this case called copy-protection) and other forms of works, including databases, have suitable provisions for this. Of particular interest is the protection of computer programs and databases, which may also be protected by a database right.

Computer programs

Computer programs and preparatory design material for computer programs are a form of literary work. Section 3(1) Copyright, Designs and Patents Act 1988 states:

...'literary work' means any work, other than a dramatic or musical work, which is written, spoken or sung, and accordingly includes -

(i) a table or compilation (other than a database);(ii) a computer program;

(iii) preparatory design material for a computer program; and

(iv) a database

For the purposes of copyright a computer programme is original in the sense that it is the author's own intellectual creation. The Act simply requires that a computer program is original, unlike the Directive which uses the above formula.

The basic rules on the restricted acts and infringement apply to computer programs as with other forms of literary work. However, there are some special rules as to what constitutes an adaptation of a compute program and there are some specific permitted acts that apply to computer programs (back-up copies, decompilation, observing, studying and testing and other acts permitted to lawful users). Rules as to ownership are the same as other original works but the nature of the software industry means that many computer programs and other items of software are created by consultants and self-employed persons.

There are no significant issues with respect of duplicate copying of computer programs but non-textual copying can cause problems, such as where an alleged infringer has written a new computer program to emulate the operational and functional aspects of an existing program, sometimes using a completely different computer programming language.

One case that highlights this is Nova Productions Ltd v Mazooma Games Ltd (2007) where the defendant created a computer game which had some similar features to the claimant's game such as the 'power cue'. Both games were based on the game of pool with coloured balls and a green baize table with pockets. The main finding here was that there was no infringement. Although there were similarities, there was no allegation of copying the claimant's program source code. merely emulating an existing program without more does not infringe. the claim was not sufficiently specific to cover copying of the detailed architecture of the claimant's program and merely amounted to a claim to copying general ideas. Jacob LJ said:

'If protection for such general ideas as are relied on here were conferred by the law, copyright would become an instrument of oppression rather than the incentive for creation which it is intended to be. protection would have moved to cover works merely inspired by others, to ideas themselves'.

Databases

It should be noted that although 'computer program' is not defined in the act, there is a definition of 'database' that applies equally to copyright databases and databases protected by the database right even though the two rights are different.

The main definition of a database is that a database is a collection of independent works, data or other materials which are arranged in a systematic or methodical way and are individually accessible by electronic or other means.

Databases can be electronic or other wise. For example, a card index arranged alphabetically would fall within the definition. The contents themselves need not be works of copyright (data or other materials) but if the contents are protected by copyright or other rights, such rights are not prejudiced by the protection of a database as a database.

For the database right to subsist, there must be substantial investment (in terms of human, technical or financial resources) in the obtaining, verification or presentation of the contents of the database. The repeated and systematic extraction and re-utilisation of insubstantial parts of the contents of a database may infringe the database right where, cumulatively. these acts amount to an extraction and/or re-utilisation of a substantial part of the contents of a database measured qualitatively and/or quantitatively.

Patents and computer software

Certain things are excluded from the meaning of 'invention' for the purposes of patent law. the list of things is not exhaustive, nor is there any deducible common logic between the things excluded. Computer programs, as such, are excluded as are business methods and mental acts. Where there is a 'technical effect' this may overcome the exception but where a computer program only performs other excluded matter, this will not count as a valid technical effect, for example, in the case of a business method implemented by a computer program. The main statute covering this area is Article 52 of the European Patent Convention. This states:

(1) European patents shall be granted for any inventions, in all fields of technology, provided that they are new, involve an inventive step and are susceptible of industrial application.
(2) The following in particular shall not be regarded as inventions within the meaning of paragraph 1:

(a) discoveries, scientific theories and mathematical methods;
(b) aesthetic creations;
(c) schemes, rules and methods for performing mental acts, playing games or doing business, and programs for computers;
(d) presentation of information.

(3) paragraph 2 shall exclude the patentability of the subject matter or activities referred to therein only to the extent to

which a European patent application or European patent relates to such subject matter or activities as such.

Design law and computer generated images

Before the harmonisation of registered design law in Europe and the introduction of the Community design, it was almost impossible to register computer graphics as designs in the UK. The definition of 'design' and 'product' under the harmonising directive and the Community Design Regulation changed this. The key statute here is Article 3 (a) and (b) of the Community Design Regulation (Article (1a) and (b) of the Directive on the legal protection of designs)

(a) 'design' means the appearance of the whole or a part of a product resulting from the features of, in particular, the lines, contours, colours, shape, texture and/or materials of the product itself and/or its ornamentation;

(b) 'product' means any industrial or handicraft item, including *inter alia* parts intended to be assembled into a complex product, packaging, get up, graphic symbols and typographic typefaces, but excluding computer programs.

Although computer programs are expressly excluded, this does not extend to symbols and images generated by computer programs. Also, fonts, being typographical typefaces, are capable of protection.

Please note the changes to design law and also patents following The UK's departure from the EU, as outlined in the chapter on Design law.

****

187

Ch. 14

Other Forms of Protection

Intellectual Property (IP) covers a wide range of subject areas and you may find that you can protect your idea by another right.

Companies House

Companies House deals with the registration and provision of company information.

Registering company names

Companies House is responsible for company registration in Great Britain. Company law is different from trade mark law. You cannot stop someone using a trade mark, which is the same or similar to yours, just by registering your name with Companies House. The IPO cannot guarantee that the name of a company accepted for registration at Companies House is acceptable by the IPO as a registered trade mark. The company name may not qualify as a trade mark because, for example:

- It is not considered distinctive,
- It is a descriptive word or term
- It may indicate geographical origin,
- It may already be registered in someone else's name

The following examples of company names would not be accepted as trade marks:

- Trutworthy plumbers
- Cheap insurance

In the same way, a trade mark, which is a word, might not be accepted for registration at Companies House.

Company Names Tribunal

The Tribunal adjudicates in disputes about opportunistic company name registrations.

Conditional access technology

For encrypted broadcasts and transmissions, you may need Conditional access technology. Conditional access technology generally refers to technical measures, such as smart cards or other decoders, which allow users to view or listen to encrypted broadcasts.

Some broadcasts and other transmissions are in an encrypted form so that they can only be seen by a person who has the right decoding equipment, a system usually used when broadcasters wish to charge recipients of the transmission.

On payment of the appropriate fee a person is given or is entitled to use a decoder and view the transmission. In the same way that people make illegal copies of copyright works, they may make unauthorised smart cards or other decoding equipment with the intention of selling them in competition with the legitimate decoders, and so depriving the broadcaster or cable operator of the payments that would normally be paid for reception of the transmissions.

A Guide to Copyright and Intellectual Property Law-The Easyway

The law therefore sets out in what circumstances it is illegal to make and sell or otherwise deal in unauthorised decoders: there may be criminal as well as civil penalties. If you use an illegal decoder to receive broadcasts you're not entitled to, you may be committing an offence.

The Telecommunications UK Fraud Forum (TUFF) represents some makers of encrypted transmissions who are concerned about illegal decoders in the United Kingdom.

Copy protection devices

For copyright material issued to the public in an electronic form, you may decide to use technical measures so that it is not possible to make a copy of your material, that is, it is copy-protected.

It is also possible for you to use other technological measures to prevent other types of illegal uses of copyright material.

Where you have sold copies that are protected by technical measures, you may have the right to take action against a person who gets round or who makes, sells or otherwise deals in devices or means specifically designed or adapted to get round, the technical measures.

The right to take action is equivalent to the rights you have when suing for infringement of your copyright in the civil courts. Criminal offences may also apply to those who deal in the means to get round technical measures

Confidentiality agreements (CDAs)

It is important that you do not make your invention public before you apply to patent it, because this may mean that you cannot patent it, or it may make your patent invalid.

190

However, that does not mean that you must never discuss your invention with anyone else. For example, you can discuss it with qualified (registered) lawyers, solicitors and patent attorneys because anything you say to or show them is legally privileged. This means it is in confidence and they will not tell anyone else.

Alternatively, you may need to discuss your invention with someone else before you apply for a patent – such as a patent adviser or consultant, or an inventor-support organisation. If so, a Non-Disclosure Agreement (NDA) can help. NDAs are also known as confidentiality agreements and confidentiality-disclosure agreements (CDA).

No single NDA will work in every situation. This means that you must think carefully about what to include in your NDA. You may want to consult a qualified lawyer or patent attorney if you are thinking about discussing your invention with someone else and are considering using a non-disclosure agreement.

Plant breeders rights

If you have created a new variety of plant or seed, you may be able to protect it at The Plant Variety Rights Office and Seeds Division in the Department for Environment Food and Rural Affairs (DEFRA).

Publication right

Publication right gives rights broadly equivalent to copyright, to a person who publishes for the first time a literary, dramatic, musical or artistic work or a film in which copyright has expired. However, there is one major difference, publication right only lasts for 25 years from the year of publication of the previously unpublished material.

It is important to note that the owner of publication right is the person who first publishes the unpublished material in which copyright has expired which will not necessary be the original owner of the copyright in the work.

This right should not be confused with the protection afforded published editions

Protection abroad

If you want to protect your IP abroad you will generally need to apply for protection in the countries which you want your IP to have effect. Except particularly in the case of Copyright and other limited circumstances, your UK IP rights do not give you automatic protection abroad .

Trade secrets

You should consider keeping something as a trade secret if:

- it is not appropriate for intellectual property (IP) protection
- you want to keep it secret or-
- you want protection to extend beyond the term of a patent

If it would be difficult to copy the process, construction or formulation from your product itself, a trade secret may give you the protection you need.

However, a trade secret does not stop anyone from inventing the same process or product independently, and can be difficult to keep.

The law of confidentiality protects trade secrets. To keep trade secrets protected, you must establish that the information is confidential, and ensure that anyone you tell about it signs a

Non-Disclosure agreement (NDA). If they then tell anyone about it, this is a breach of confidence and you can take legal action against them.

****

Useful Addresses and Websites

Chartered Society of Designers

www.csd.org.uk

Chartered Institute of Patent Attorneys

www.cipa.org.uk

Companies House

www.companieshouse.gov.uk

England and Wales

Companies House

Crown Way

Cardiff CF14 3UZ

Espacenet (search existing patents)

www.epo.org/searching/free/espacenet.html

European Patent Office

www.epo.org

FICPI-UK

The National United Kingdom association of the International Federation of Intellectual Property Attorneys.

www.ficpi.org.uk

Intellectual Property Office

Concept House

Cardiff Road

Newport
South Wales
NP10 8QQ
Telephone 0300 300 2000
Fax +44 (0)1633 817777
www.ipo.gov.uk

Institute of Patentees and Inventors

theipi.org.uk

Institute of Trade Mark Attorneys

www.itma.org.uk

Nominet (Domain name searches)

www.nominet.org.uk

Office for Harmonization in the Internal market (Trade marks and Designs)

www.oami.europa.eu

World Intellectual Property Organization

www.wipo.int

Index